JOURNEY THROUGH HALLOWED GROUND

JOURNEY THROUGH HALLOWED GROUND

BIRTHPLACE OF THE AMERICAN IDEAL

By Andrew Cockburn
Photography by Kenneth Garrett

NATIONAL GEOGRAPHIC

WASHINGTON, D.C.

LOGGING THE OLD-FASHIONED WAY
This draft horse pulling contest draws a festive crowd. Today in
Warrenton, Virginia, draft horses are used to pull logs, just as they
were when the first pioneers came to the Piedmont. Although there
are quicker ways to log today, like mechanical skidders, horse labor
is more environmentally friendly.

CONTENTS

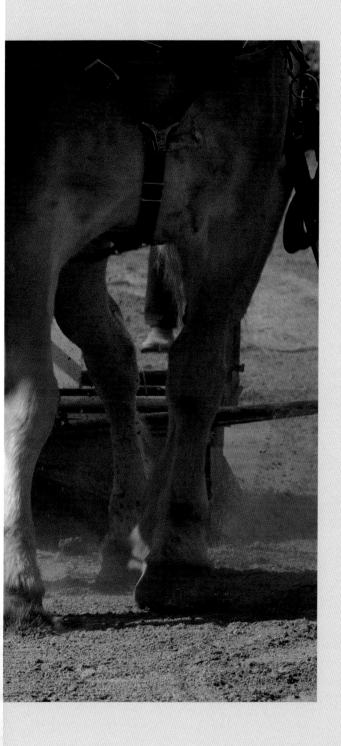

Foreword

The Journey Through Hallowed Ground became my home ground in the most serendipitous way. In 1989, simply wanting to get out of the city on a beautiful early-summer morning, we'd set off on an aimless drive. My husband and I were foreign correspondents in those days, working for the *Wall Street Journal* in faraway cities such as Cairo, Sydney, Berlin, and London. Back in the United States on a brief home leave, we drove west out of Washington D.C., taking small byways, with no plans beyond a picnic lunch by a reach of winding creek somewhere.

Within an hour the city, the suburbs and the exurbs had given way to fields, plowed soft as corduroy or blooming in the urgent green of early corn. The farmhouses and the barns—red, white, weathered gray timbers, or miraculous jigsaws of careful drystone—settled gently into the hollows of the landscape, shaded by immense old maples or sycamores. Later, I would learn that one of those huge trees provided an escape route for John Mosby as he climbed out a bedroom window to elude pursuing Union troops. I would come to know that one of the houses we passed had been home to President Monroe. And I would walk fields haunted by the ghosts of missing youths who had died believing deeply in freedom, or in duty.

But that first day I had no idea how dense and how deep the history of this remarkable stretch of ground could be. What captivated me first of all were not links with great figures or great moments of American history, but the remarkable stewardship of land and landscape that had kept the templates of ordinary American lives. When we came over a gentle rise of ground and entered the tiny village of Waterford, Virginia, population 250, I was transported by an extraordinary sense of connection with the past.

"Settled in 1733" said a sign at the village edge. Its modest houses, no more than about 80 in all, pressed cozily together, anchored at one end by an old brick grist mill that had once been the settlement's reason for being. The village's footprint had remained small within enfolding pasturelands, grazed by cows and yielding crops as they had for more than two centuries. There were icehouses still standing, evoking a kind of hard, shared, communal toil lost in most contemporary experience. There were root cellars and well pumps that told of a way of life where nothing came without effort, and where the bounty of the Earth—its water and its food—could not therefore be wasted in our wanton modern way. The brick church, on the rise of ground near the village's eastern edge, still bore the marks of the shots fired there in a Civil War skirmish. The one-room schoolhouse built just after that war to educate the village's African-American children was a marker on the nation's long and difficult journey toward equality and inclusion. In the cemetery, Union and Confederate dead lay buried side by side in the red clay.

I know that clay now. It is the dirt beneath my fingernails when I come in from tending my garden. Just a few years after that serendipitous summer drive, we moved from London into a small stucco cottage that dated from 1810. I have come to know the place, in the deep and intimate ways you know a place where you begin a family, raise a child. I have learned how to work the same sticky soil that yielded food to the Catoctin Indians who lived here, and the Quakers from Pennsylvania who followed them.

Once a year, during Waterford's annual crafts fair, we open our house for tours, and I love to watch the wonder in the schoolchildren's eyes when I explain to them that the trapdoor in the kitchen ceiling was where the Quaker children who lived here in the 19th century would be put to bed, hoisted aloft on their parents' shoulders, to sleep in the warm space created by the cooking fire. I let them haul a bucket of water from the stone-lined, hand-dug well, and ask them to imagine how many buckets they would have to haul in a day to cook and bathe and launder for a family. I hand them the Union soldier's belt buckle unearthed near that well, and I see them transported as they turn it in their fingers, trying to imagine the young man who might have worn it. In 1861, many young men in Waterford were Quakers, and therefore pacifists, deeply opposed to all war. But for some, slavery was a greater evil, and so they enlisted to serve on the Union side. I tell the children that maybe the belt buckle belonged to one of those young men, and I watch them frown and consider his choices, and think about the choice that they would make if they were in his place.

None of this would be possible were it not for the stewardship of the people who lived in this house before us. They valued that old well and the kitchen trapdoor, and kept them, even though their original purpose had long since become obsolete. They were mindful people who understood that our whims—here, now, this moment—must be measured against an obligation to the past and to the future, which will unfurl into a world whose ways and wants and needs we cannot begin to predict. Because of their stewardship, and the care of hundreds like them, landscapes and buildings still exist in this remarkable region that can tell the story of how and where America happened. They have the power to transport us on the greatest adventure of all: the journey of empathy and imagination into the lives of the people—famous and unknown, humble and distinguished—who shaped this country and made us who we are.

—Geraldine Brooks

THE WARRENTON HUNT
A scarlet-jacketed fox hunter leads his hounds to the gathering spot.
First established in 1887 and recognized by 1893, this hunt is one of
the oldest in the area and provides numerous topographical challenges.

JEFFERSON'S ROCK
Overlooking the confluence of the Shenandoah and Potomac Rivers in Harpers Ferry, West Virginia, with St. Peter's Church below, the rock inspired Thomas Jefferson, for whom it was named, to extol the beauty of Virginia.

WINE COUNTRY
Rows of vines dwarf a piece of machinery at Boxwood Winery near Middleburg, Virginia. Here John Kent Cooke and his wife, Rita, are making premium wine in a region that is becoming famous for its high-quality production.

BEVERLEY MILL
Built in George Washington's day the mill, located near Thoroughfare Gap in Virginia, was gutted by fire. It provided flour for troops during the course of five wars.

THE SOUTHWEST MOUNTAINS
Located in Albemarle County, Virginia, the mountains, shrouded in fog
in this aerial view, were home to James Monroe's Ash Lawn-Highland,
Thomas Jefferson's Monticello, and James Madison's Montpelier.

MONOCACY RIVER
A graceful aqueduct carrying the Chesapeake and Ohio Canal spans the Monocacy River in northern Maryland. When Confederates attempted to blow up the bridge, the canal's lockkeeper persuaded them to destroy the earthworks only.

INVITING COUNTRYSIDE
Misty farmland near Delaplane, Virginia, in Fauquier County. This is the idyllic countryside that attracted early settlers. Today the rolling hills are still appreciated for their fertile fields and scenic views.

APPLE-PICKING TIME
Six generations have farmed the land at Stribling Orchard near
Linden, Virginia, producing fruit for almost 200 years. In addition to
pick-your-own fruit, there are vendors selling home-grown and crafted
goods at the annual Applefest.

THE ROUND BARN
Located near Cashtown, Pennsylvania, the northern end of the historic Hallowed Ground route, the barn marks the spot where Lee obtained supplies before marching on to the Battle of Gettysburg.

THE CHESAPEAKE AND OHIO CANAL
A barge polls away from the dock on the canal at Great Falls, Virginia.
When ready, the mules at right will pull the barge as they once did,
enabling finished goods to be transported upriver from Washington,
D.C., to Cumberland, Maryland, and raw materials back again.

PRIMEVAL LANDSCAPE
The Potomac River winds past the Catoctin Mountain Range. Equipped with boats, early English settlers chose the relative ease of river passage over arduous trail-breaking land travel in the densely forested Piedmont.

CHAPTER ONE

First Land

First Land

"THEN WE ASKED HIM WHAT WAS BEYOND THE MOUNTAINES,

HE ANSWERED THE SUNNE."

—JOHN SMITH OF HIS 1608 CONVERSATION WITH A MONACAN

Until late in life, Thomas Jefferson was never happier than when riding the 5,000 acres of his beloved Monticello. The plantation perched on an 850-foot peak in the Southwest Mountains, overlooking the Piedmont foothills that stretched out from the Blue Ridge Mountains to the west. Here, he told a friend, he could "ride above the storms" and "look down into the workhouse of nature, to see her clouds, hail, snow,

rain, thunder, all fabricated at our feet! And the glorious Sun, when rising as if out of a distant water, just gilding the tops of the mountains, and giving life to all nature!" This land, he insisted, was "the Eden of the United States for soil, climate, navigation, and health."

The country he surveyed with such delight stretched east from the Appalachians to the point where the rivers drop down over rock-strewn rapids onto the flat coastal plain. To the west rose the rugged landscape of what would one day become West Virginia; to the north of the Potomac, the Blue Ridge mountain chain extended into the South and Catoctin Mountains of Maryland and southern Pennsylvania.

Often enough, Jefferson would have to leave Monticello and head north to handle matters of the new nation's business. The ride to Washington took four days, with three overnight stops at the houses of friends, such as James Madison's Montpelier a few miles outside Orange. In the general absence of highway signs or paved roads, it was sometimes easy to get lost. After leaving Orange, Jefferson

warned his daughter Martha, "Be very attentive to the roads, as they begin to be difficult to find."

Nowadays we subdue geography with concrete and tarmac, but in Jefferson's time roads—unpaved, of course—still had to follow the contours and obstacles of the landscape. Travelers heading up the Blue Ridge searched for the place where the rivers could be forded in safety. The route that Jefferson looked for beyond Orange, for example, took him across the Germanna Ford on the Rapidan River and on up via Culpeper County, where he would lodge with his friend John Strode, to Norman's Ford on the Rappahannock.

Officially known as Route 15 today, this route along the ford line was once more evocatively termed the Old Carolina Road. In the 18th century, when it became the haunt of highway robbers, people started calling it Rogue's Road. Not long before, it had guided Iroquois hunting parties coming south in search of furs to trade with the Europeans. The stretch running from Gettysburg, Pennsylvania, to Monticello, Virginia, encompasses some of the nation's most historic sites.

A 1630 VELLUM MAP SHOWS KNOWN SETTLEMENTS AND RIVER PASSAGES.

Stegara

Haſſuinſa

Tanxſnitania

Shachaconia

MANNAHOACKS.

Mahaſkahod

W   H   A

Martoughquuunk
Vteuſtank
Accoqueck
Seebbeck
Maſſawoteck
Soccobeck   Quiyough
Avaſkenoans
Chekopiſſowo   Waconiaſk
Monanaſk   Cuttatawomen
Naudtanghtacundt
Anrenapeugh   Aſſuweſka   Patawo meck
Papiſcone   Mattacimt
Kerahocack   Pamacocack
N.   Ozaiawomen
Piſſaſeck   Nuſſamek
Nawacatz   Mataughqua
Mangoraca   ment   Pamaco
Wecuppom   Nuſhemouck   cack
Matchopick   Cinquag
Piſſacoack   Potapoco   teck   Tauxenent
Winlack   Caſowontol   Moyaons   Namaſſingakent
Acquack   Aſſaomeck
Tantuc   Cecomocomoco   Teſſamatuck
quaſk   Macaraweo Wighcocomoco   Woſameus
Poykemkac   Acquaſkack   Mattpament   Nacotchtanck
Nawnautceu   Acquintanac   Waſhaweas
Toppahanock   ſuck
Monunauk   Ozaia
Pawtuxunt   flu.   Pawtuxunt
Quomocac
Opanient   Rikards Cliffes

Cheſapeack Bay.

Powels Iles

Bornes point

But men and women had trodden this path long before any rogues or traders appeared on the scene. On the banks of the Rappahannock at Norman's Ford, for example, Jefferson was standing on a vast swath of history. Artifacts range from deadly arrowheads and sharp spear points dropped 9,000 years ago during the Archaic period to trading beads of fine white kaolin shipped over from England by 17th-century settlers, along with pipe stems, pottery shards, an early 18th-century Spanish coin, buttons, and hundreds of other objects. Unearthed today from one small section of the riverbank by an archaeologist's patient trowel, these revealing mementoes of other ages combine to make the spot a four-dimensional snapshot, an image of time as well as space. As nowhere else in America, this phenomenon applies to the entire landscape stretching from Charlottesville in Albemarle County, Virginia, north to Gettysburg in Adams County, Pennsylvania—a wide corridor distinguished by its unparalled concentration of American heritage as the Journey Through Hallowed Ground. In this region, our past is as visible and tangible a part of the landscape as the green fields and woods carpeting the soft contours of the hills and valleys.

LONG A GUIDE FOR TRAVELERS, RIVER CROSSINGS WOULD in time direct the movements of warring armies. One day when Union and Confederate cavalries clashed at Kelly's Ford, along the Rappahannock, a soldier took one of his lead bullets, flattened and pierced it to make a sinker for a fishing line, then dropped or lost it close by the buried 8,000-year-old arrowheads. It provides an evocative echo of the moment when a young man in the middle of a huge and bloody war decided to catch himself some supper.

That soldier in uniform would have looked appropriate, because nature had molded Jefferson's "Eden" to be a perfect killing field, complete with level open country on which to fight battles, mountain ranges to mask troop movements, as well as lush breadbaskets for feeding men and horses. "You cannot understand the history of the Piedmont without understanding the land, and what has shaped it," observed geologist Lynn S. Fichter of James Madison University, and his comment can apply to all this Hallowed Ground. "Geology imposes on us humans vastly more than most of us acknowledge, or realize." This landscape, the stage on which the most vital episodes in our history have been acted out, was shaped by dramatic and violent movements of the Earth's crust long before life appeared.

FROM A BILLION YEARS AGO, THE LAND WAS REPEATEDLY convulsed as tectonic plates floated across the Earth's soft mantle to collide, push up mountain ranges, rip apart, collide again, and once again separate, leaving oceans in their path. Two hundred and fifty million years ago the last of these collisions, known to geologists as the Alleghenian orogeny, built a towering mountain range that brought up from deep inside the earth fragments of all the earlier mountain-building events in the region. The present-day Blue Ridge rocks are the deepest roots of a billion-year-old event, whereas the Piedmont contains the roots of two different mountains that existed between 485 million and 345 million years ago. The present-day valley and ridge are the sediments deposited from erosion of those mountains. All these rocks have been shuffled like a deck of cards, so no rock is in its original location, and rocks that are older are sometimes stacked on rocks that are younger. As Africa ripped away and the Atlantic Ocean emerged to fill the gap, the Blue Ridge towered over the ancient coastline, its peaks soaring as high as the mighty Himalaya today. Eons of time have eroded that awesome range down to the familiar ridges, carpeted with the seasonally shifting canopies of countless hardwoods. Meanwhile, materials wearing off the shrinking peaks spread out into a new coastal plain.

This history of geologic spasms is recorded in the mosaic of rocks from various ages underpinning the area today. Whereas much of the American landscape is based on a uniform foundation, a walk along these streambeds quickly reveals dozens of different types of stone, from granite to sandstone to quartz and more. Such variety has always had a direct impact on those who lived here. For example, Monticello and Montpelier sat on rich productive soil formed from a 540-million-year-old lava flow called Catoctin Ridge. This iron-rich rock, when weathered by water and atmospheric gases, turns into the red soil so typical of the region.

A FISHERMAN CASTS HIS LINE downstream from an old fishing weir on the Potomac River south of Shepherdstown, West Virginia. These fish lures, built with rocks by Native Americans, still exist in rivers throughout the corridor. The weir consists of two tightly packed walls of stones extending from opposite banks and pointing downstream together to form a V. Around the point where they converge, flowing water is forced over the top of the rocks, churning and becoming aerated as the water spills over. Fish, attracted by the aerated water, would swim toward this point and into traps laid by the Native Americans. As river traffic increased with settlement, many weirs were removed, however, many are still visible today.

THE WESTERN WORLD
This 1584 map shows the Western world, including Wingandekoa (Virginia). Spanish and French colonists already had settlements in North America, predating English colonists by almost a century.

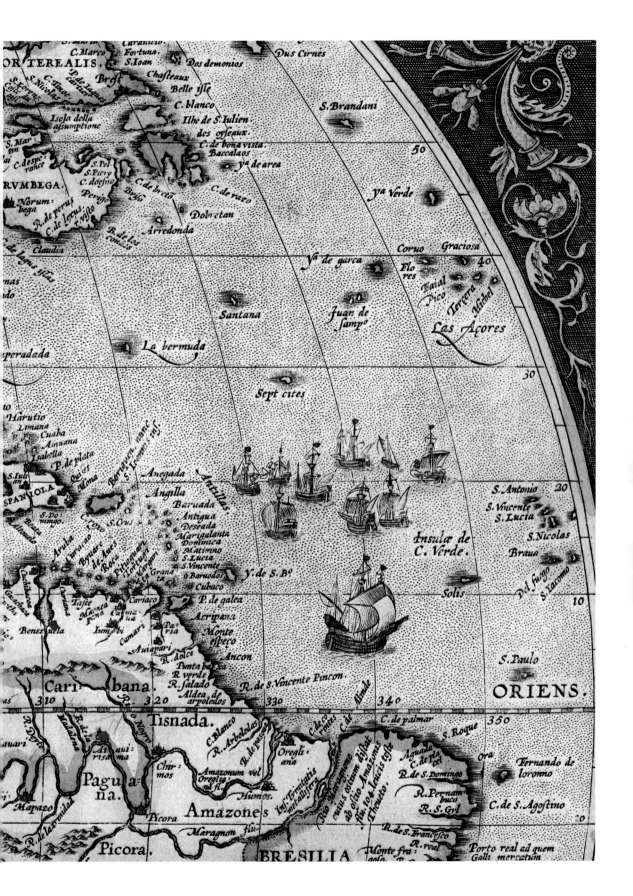

The Blue Ridge itself was long a barrier to the westward expansion of English settlers, which is why there are almost no grand colonial mansions—so much a part of this region's landscape—west of the Blue Ridge. Later these mountains channeled the movements of the Civil War armies between the two enemy capitals of Washington, D.C., and Richmond, Virginia, compressing the struggle for an entire continent into one comparatively small battleground. The mountains were the barrier that held the early European colonists back from probing the interior of the New World.

JOHN SMITH, THE INITIAL LEADER OF THE JAMESTOWN settlement down on the Tidewater, took only a tentative look at the unknown world above the rapids of the rivers that flow into the Chesapeake Bay and reported that it seemed a "faire, fertill, well-watred countrie." He knew nothing about the territory to the north and west, or of the inland inhabitats he encountered, the Monacan Indians, who spoke an entirely different language from the Powhatan Indians of the coastal plains. What little he did

ALEXANDER SPOTSWOOD, GOVERNOR of Virginia from 1710 to 1722, led a group of adventurers known as "the Knights of the Golden Horseshoe" across the Piedmont and over the Blue Ridge mountains, discovering the state's central valley, the Shenandoah.

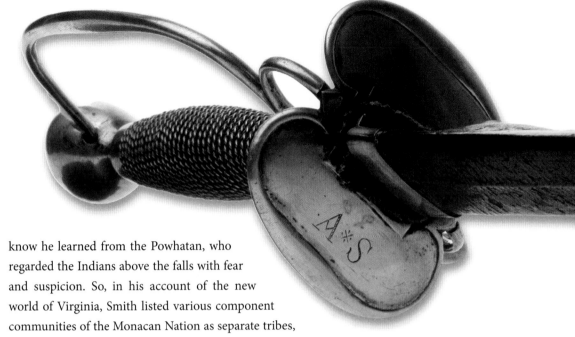

know he learned from the Powhatan, who regarded the Indians above the falls with fear and suspicion. So, in his account of the new world of Virginia, Smith listed various component communities of the Monacan Nation as separate tribes, undercounted their towns, and generally wrote off the people of the Piedmont as "barbarous" and "living ... [on] wild beests and fruits." This verdict endured as the last word on the Monacan for centuries. Only recently has it begun to dawn on experts that not only was there a very different story to be told about these people but that human history in the Hallowed Ground corridor extended back much farther than previously supposed.

THIS FORMAL, SILVER-HILTED SMALL sword, circa 1722, is attributed to Alexander Spotswood and is engraved with his initials.

IN 1998, ABOUT FOUR MILES EAST OF NORMAN'S FORD, archaeologists surveying ahead of a planned expansion of Route 3 chanced to dig under a grove of cedars and came across an ancient work site: a quarry hewn out of the rock and surrounded by roughly 700,000 stone flakes and tools. About 11,500 years ago, as the glaciers of the last ice age were still retreating up Pennsylvania (the ice never quite reached Maryland and Virginia, but it was still colder than today), someone passing by this spot was smart enough to notice that an outcrop of red sandstone was laced with veins of a yellowish rock called jasper. Hammered with a harder rock, the sandstone would disintegrate into sand, but the jasper flaked into hard sharp-edged shards—ideal as spear points for hunting mammoths and other large game. Archaeologists estimate that this quarry, a narrow shaft up to two feet wide now known as the Brook Run site, was worked for as long as 500 years.

INTO THE UNKNOWN
At Swift Run Gap, Alexander Spotswood and his Knights crossed the uncharted barrier of the Blue Ridge mountains to discover the great fertile Shenandoah Valley—a breakthrough for westward expansion.

Three thousand years later, when people started dropping spear points and arrowheads at nearby Norman's Ford, the mammoths had disappeared and the people of the area now hunted smaller game—deer, bobcats, lynx—adapting their weapons' designs accordingly. To improve the grazing for the animals they hunted, these peoples regularly set fire to the forest undergrowth while cultivating various nutritious plants in gardens.

At some point between 1,000 and 2,000 years ago, they started taking further steps to improve their environment. As well as "managing" the forests by selective burning, they began systematically replanting stretches of woodland with useful trees that would give them chestnuts, beechnuts, hickory nuts, butternuts, and persimmons. Europeans who later gazed in appreciation at the "virgin" forests, with their gratifying quantities of fruit and nut trees, little understood that they were actually looking at a superb example of land management.

Then, about a thousand years before our time, came a really momentous change. Maize, or corn, the product of a remarkable feat of bioengineering somewhere in what is now Mexico, finally made its way into the Piedmont and surrounding lands. Life in the area was transformed. Whereas in earlier times people had been spread more or less evenly across the hills, they now clustered on the floodplains of the rivers in large settlements, close by their fields. Assured of

THIS SHORT, DOUBLE BRASS-BARRELED dog-lock pistol was manufactured in England. The circa 1700 early pocket piece most likely was in the possession of an upper class settler.

a steady source of food from the new crop, they seem to have placed less importance on hunting, even though tending the maize fields probably involved a lot more work, since ground for new fields had to be cleared continually as the soil became depleted. According to Fredericksburg archaeologist Mike Carmody, "You see a decline in quality of the tools they were making at this time compared to what they had been making a few thousand years earlier, almost as if it didn't matter any more. They were even using quartz, which can look a bit like cheap plastic."

Around the same time as corn cultivation began to spread in the Piedmont, a new nation moved in, the Monacan. According to the history passed down through the generations from father to son and finally recorded on paper by an early European explorer, they originally migrated from what is now Ohio, over the mountains of West Virginia, and eastward into Maryland and Virginia, "driven by an Enemy from the Northwest." They arrived to find the original inhabitants, as the explorer noted, "feeding only upon raw flesh and fish, until these taught them to plant Corn, and shewed them the use of it."

Archaeologists can confirm today that a new people did indeed arrive on the scene about A.D. 1000, thanks to carbon-14 dating of bones in the burial mounds in which the Monacan deposited their dead. Some of these mounds were used for hundreds of years—layer upon layer of skeletons, each covered with earth or stones, until they grew to be 20 feet high and 40 feet around. A mound on the Rapidan River in Orange County that was excavated in the 1970s and 1980s held the bones of some 2,000 people. Intriguingly, they had been jumbled together deliberately. According to Debra Gold, a professor of anthropology at St. Cloud State University in Minnesota, who conducted extensive research on these remains, "one possibility is that they wanted to show that in death we are all equal, which in turn suggests that in life these people were not equal."

THE PIEDMONT POSES A CHALLENGE FOR ARCHAEOLOGISTS. In many places the soil is so acidic that artifacts such as bones disintegrate in a short space of time. But the sheer quantity of bones packed together in the mounds, according to Gold, "created their own environment, overcoming the acidity and ensuring their preservation." Unlike many other cultures, including that

A BRITISH CARVED POWDER horn dates from circa 1700 and shows contrasting scenes of the times. In the middle of the horn an Indian is depicted scalping a kilted Scot, while at the bottom, a crown is held aloft over a gentleman riding a horse.

NATIVE AMERICAN
Adorned with stripes of red and black body paint, New World natives mystified and intrigued settlers as well as Old World residents. This engraving by John White was published by Theodore de Bry in 1587.

Habit of a Nobleman of Virginia.

DON THARPE

EVERYTHING THAT SURROUNDS ME MAKES ME FEEL LIKE I BELONG HERE. THE CHANGING SEASONS MEAN SO MUCH, AND THE LANDSCAPE OF THE WOODLANDS, AND THE FOOTHILLS MERGING INTO THE MOUNTAINS.

Don Tharpe, founder of the Liberty Heritage Society which operates a museum in Old Town Warrenton, Virginia, has devoted a significant portion of his life to researching the Piedmont, especially its natives peoples, early settlers, and conflicts. His work as a historian, collector, and art historian has contributed significantly to knowledge of American history. He has individually led an unprecedented effort to rediscover the Piedmont region.

"I'm a seventh-generation Piedmont Tharpe, beginning with my Revolutionary War grandfathers, John and Thomas. John fought in the Second Virginia Regiment and was wounded, while Thomas served with Lafayette and fought against the English cavalry commander Tarleton.

"I was born in Washington, D.C., but I'm proud to say I've lived in the Piedmont since I was six months old, apart from a few years spent away at college. I've always been interested in history. When I was eight years old my mother found me out in the yard digging

Don Tharpe,
Piedmont historian

with a stick. She asked me what I was doing and I told her I was an archaeologist. I found my first arrowhead when I was nine, on my grandfather's farm. Since 1999 I've been digging at Ludwell Park (the historic property of the colonial magnate Philip Ludwell) and have found more than 20,000 artifacts. The dig at Norman's Ford has turned up another 15,000. I spent many years looking for Civil War artifacts, but lately I've been more attracted to the Native American era, plus the period of contact (with Europeans) and the first hundred years of settlement. That was a time of great hardships for the Native Americans at the hands of the English who were coming to settle in Virginia. Much of that history is forgotten now, but in fact it was well covered in books written at the time, such as Robert Beverley's *History and Present State of Virginia*, published in 1705.

"Everything that surrounds me makes me feel like I belong here. The changing seasons mean so much, and the landscape of the woodlands, and the foothills merging into the mountains. This is the place I've always lived. I cannot be taken out of here."

of their Powhatan neighbors, the Monacan usually did not bury artifacts with their dead; so all Gold had to work with when she began examining remains from 3 of the mounds—there were 13 altogether that we know about in the Piedmont—were the bones themselves. It was an intriguing exercise in archaeological detective work, but slowly, long-dead Monacans began to take form again. Gold found, for example, that maize had been something of a mixed blessing. "They started to get cavities in their teeth because of eating that starchy, sticky grain," which the bones told her they consumed in large quantities. These farmers and innovators were the people dismissed by John Smith as "barbarous."

Farther north lived Iroquoian-speaking Indians who did not observe the practice of burying their dead in mounds. These peoples were decimated early on by diseases such as smallpox and influenza, which traveled to North America with the Spanish even before 1600. Realignment and migration in the later 17th century brought the Shawnee through Pennsylvania, but the Powhatan and Monacan peoples represented the Native Americans with the longest lasting presence in the territory of the Hallowed Ground once European settlers arrived.

The German explorer John Lederer, who spent time among the Monacan some 60 years later, wrote that he had been present "at several of their consultations and debates, and to my admiration have heard some of their Seniors deliver themselves with as much Judgment and Eloquence as I should have expected from men of Civil education and Literature." Given the evident sophistication of his neighbors, it is not surprising that the Powhatan chief on the coastal plain should have done everything he could to prevent contact between them and the English, especially as he saw that these visitors from across the sea could free him from depending on the Monacan for supplies of a vital commodity: copper. Just as the chief was telling the English that it was not worth their while to travel upriver to the land of the Monacan, and certainly not to the distant "Quirank"—the Indian name for the Blue Ridge—one of his men whispered to an Englishman that in fact Quirank was their source of copper.

This was a significant revelation. The Powhatan prized copper as the ultimate symbol of power and wealth. Chiefs were buried with it. Before the English arrived, they had been forced to depend on the Monacan to trade the priceless metal from their mines in the Blue

NAMED FOR THE HEALTH AND well-being the word evokes, Salubria (opposite, top) is a Georgian manor house built in 1742. Its stately presence can be observed just off the Old Carolina Road at Stevensburg, Virginia. Given by the Grayson family to the Germanna Foundation in more recent times, it serves as an example of the type of home the early gentry would have owned. An arched stairwell (opposite, bottom) ascends from the entrance hall.

SOME 20 MILES UPSTREAM FROM

the treacherous falls of the Rappahannock, fishermen try their luck at Kelly's Ford in midsummer low water. One of the traversing places for Indians following the old Iroquois trail, Kelly's Ford enabled them to move north and south by wading across. Other fordable streams and rivers were commonly used by early settlers whose seagoing vessels could not progress beyond the fall lines. Kelly's Ford later served as the crossing point for the Old Carolina Road, was the site of a major Civil War engagement, and is now skirted by Route 15, the major route through the historic Journey Through Hallowed Ground corridor.

Ridge, where copper continued to be extracted until as recently as 1944. As it so happens, most of the Monacan burial mounds that we know about were sited close to these copper deposits, a possible indication of the importance their builders accorded this resource. So important, in fact, was copper in the politics and economy of the area that Jeffrey L. Hantman, an anthropologist at the University of Virginia, suggests that the copper trade played a crucial role in the fate of the Jamestown colony and by extension the whole future history of Virginia.

Hantman, whose research has corrected much of Smith's misinformation about the Monacan, points out that Smith and his men could call on a limitless supply of the metal from mines in England and Europe, an asset that the colony's cynical commander was quick to appreciate. By trading corn for copper, the Powhatan ruler gained wealth with which to secure the loyalty of petty chieftains in his empire and cut out the Monacan, who, according to Hantman, "may have been an unpredictable and perhaps dominating exchange partner." This could explain why this ruler allowed the colonists to survive at a time when they were few, sick, and hungry and could easily have been wiped out in the same way as earlier English and Spanish settlements along the coast.

Although the Powhatan thought they could take advantage of the English, the Monacan seem to have had a more realistic view. In July 1608, the year after he first arrived in Virginia, Smith led a 12-man expedition up the Rappahannock. Before long they were ambushed with a shower of arrows. Firing back, they hit one of the attackers in the knee. After restraining Mosco, their Powhatan interpreter, from beating the wounded man's brains out, the English gave the captive, whose name was Amoroleck, first aid and questioned him. In Smith's account of the conversation, "We asked him how many worlds he did know, he replyed, he knew no more but that which was under the skie that covered him, which were the Powhatans, with the Monacans, and the Massowomecks [another name for the Iroquois] that were higher up in the mountains. Then we asked him what was beyond the mountaines, he answered the Sunne." When he was asked why his group had attacked the English, he answered that "they heard we were a people come from under the world, to take their world from them."

EVENTS OVER THE FOLLOWING CENTURIES SEEMED TO vindicate Amoroleck's prophetic assessment, as an ever growing flood of settlers from Europe poured west, lured by the promise of cheap or free land. Forests and cornfields that had sustained the Indians for so long were eliminated in favor of tobacco, a hugely profitable cash crop. Unfortunately it also had an exhausting effect on the soil, thereby encouraging settlers to move on to fresh land, along with their workforce of slaves, the first of whom arrived from Africa in 1619. A hundred years after the founding of Jamestown, the coastal Indian tribes were largely dispersed, but for a time the barrier of the fall line, which barred the interior to oceangoing ships, preserved the Piedmont for the Monacan. As late as 1750, says Karenne Wood, a member of the Monacan Tribal Council and a historian of her people, "it was still our land. We were farming, growing corn, as well as growing tobacco and selling it to the English."

In 1669, Governor William Berkeley of Virginia commissioned German explorer John Lederer to travel beyond the western mountains in search of the Pacific Ocean, which many believed lay not far beyond. In March of that year Lederer crossed the Piedmont and became the first European to reach the Blue Ridge. In contrast

to the Tidewater, already mostly cleared of forests and Indians, this land still looked the way it had for centuries past (and in places still does). "Great herds of Red and Fallow Deer I daily saw feeding," he wrote later, "and on the hill-sides, Bears crashing Mast like swine. Small Leopards have I seen in the Woods, but never any [mountain] Lions, though their skins are much worn by Indians. The Wolves in these parts are so ravenous, that I often in the night feared my horse would be devoured by them.... Beaver and Otter I met with at every River that I passed; and the woods are full of Grey Foxes."

The Monacan, with whom Lederer remained on friendly terms during the voyages of exploration that ultimately took him down into North Carolina, were still struggling to maintain their way of life, but they were under increasing pressure both from white settlers advancing west toward the mountains and Iroquois pushing down from the northern stretch of the Hallowed Ground corridor in search of furs to trade to the Europeans. Gradually, they slipped from the pages of colonial history, a chronicle with increasingly sparse footnotes of scattered, inevitably futile uprisings, broken treaties, and increasing isolation.

Ever inquisitive, in the 1780s Thomas Jefferson excavated an Indian burial mound on his property, recalling how when he was a child a party of Indians had gone six miles out of their way to mourn at this site, "with expressions which were construed to be those of sorrow," before continuing on their way. He had no trouble in believing that

they were on their way to extinction. "Spiritous liquors, the small-pox, war, and an abridgment of territory," he wrote at that time in his *Notes on the State of Virginia*, "had committed terrible havock among them, which [re]generation, under the obstacles [they face] was not likely to make good." Jefferson assumed as a matter of course that this people had "lived principally on the spontaneous productions of nature." Clearly the Indians' rich legacy of carefully tended forests and cornfields had already been forgotten.

Their own history tells a story with important differences. "We didn't go away," says Karenne Wood, co-author of *The Monacan Indians: Our Story.* As she points out, in many areas these original Virginians adapted to the ways of the new arrivals, just as the settlers learned from them how to grow corn and clean their teeth with twigs of dogwood. "There are land records from Orange County in the 18th century where the farmers have names that are Indian. Indians were raising tobacco and selling it for shipment to England. Most of all, we just stayed out of the way and retreated into the mountains."

Dwindling in numbers, but never dying out, the Monacan hung on in their remote hideaways. Some moved north and westward, joined by the Tuscarora of North Carolina, and migrated through Pennsylvania and eventually to Canada, where they merged with the Cayuga, part of the Iroquois Confederacy. Others remained

ANCESTRAL OFFERINGS
Johnny Rocca, a Tuscarora Indian chief, leads other Native Americans
in an offering ceremony to their ancestors at a native burial mound
near Leesburg, Virginia.

KARENNE WOOD

IT'S CRITICAL ... NOT TO VIEW THE LAND JUST IN TERMS OF RESOURCES THAT
CAN BE EXTRACTED. YOU HAVE TO THINK ABOUT GIVING THINGS BACK,
PRESERVING THEM FOR THE FUTURE GENERATIONS THAT WILL COME AFTER US.

Karenne Wood is a member of the Tribal Council of the Monacan Indian Nation. She is also a published poet and the director of the Virginia Indian Heritage Program at the Virginia Foundation for the Humanities.

"There could be no place more important to us than this land. This is our homeland, the place where our ancestors are buried. It would be wrong to say that the land belongs to us—we belong to the land. That's why it is so irritating to be told that the Indians didn't deserve to own it, when we took better care of it than anyone else. As I wrote in a poem once, 'Nothing was discovered, / Everything was already loved.' I've visited other places around the world, and I can't see myself living anywhere else. You might say that it has been under occupation by out-siders for 400 years, but we can't live in the moment of contact between American Indians and colonists forever, we have to move on. The real difference is between those who view the land the same way we do and those who see it simply as something to be used. We, the native people, have our own way of relating to our homeland. We believe the land is alive and that while we interact with it, it interacts with us. In fact, native people think that the land recognizes us, like a relative.

"I worry that people today are not observing the land, not living with it, not participating in the community. That way of living is not attractive to me. I believe it's critical to pay attention to the natural cycle of things, and not to view the land just in terms of resources that can be extracted. You have to think about giving things back, preserving them for the future generations that will come after us.

"Nowadays, people are beginning to learn that the environment is something that has to be protected, but I wonder what would happen if John Smith and Powhatan came back to Virginia, what they might say about what we've done to the land. Would they recognize it? They could say: 'This place was a paradise, what happened?' Or per-haps they would be grateful that we have preserved as much as we have."

Karenne Wood, tribal council member and historian

in the Piedmont. A low point came in the 1920s, when a pseudoacademic report labeling them "Mongrel Virginians" and denying their identity as Native Americans was adopted as policy by state officials, who refused admittance of surviving Monacans to the public schools and, incredibly, dead ones from the graveyards wherever they had been buried alongside white people. The tide has turned since those dark days. The state officially recognized the Monacan as an Indian nation in 1989, and they are campaigning for the federal recognition they feel is their due.

Steadily, the Monacan are reclaiming their ancestral heritage, including their language and the bones of their ancestors previously excavated from mounds and consigned to museums. Those bones are now being respectfully reinterred at the tribal center on Bear Mountain in Amherst County, where new burial mounds are slowly growing under the trees. In 2000, the skulls of a man and a woman that had been consigned to a Monacan burial mound sometime in the 14th century and excavated in the early 20th were put into the hands of a specialist in facial reconstruction before being reinterred.

Under the expert's magic touch, the faces of this long-dead pair reappeared, lifelike, expressive—and recognizable! "That's Lincoln Johns!" was the unqualified conclusion of many tribespeople on seeing the 600-year-old head, naming a Monacan elder famous in his day for his uncanny ability to forecast the weather.

The Monacan heritage lived on in other ways, too. Jefferson, though dismissive in many ways, praised their reliance on morality to govern their societies, as opposed to laws imposed from above. "Insomuch that were it made a question, whether no law, as among the savage Americans, or too much law, as among the civilized Europeans, submits man to the greatest evil," wrote the author of the Declaration of Independence in 1782, "one who has seen both conditions of existence would pronounce it to be the last." Every July Fourth, there is a ceremony at Monticello, swearing in immigrants as new citizens of the United States of America. In 2004, the invocation at this event was given by tribal historian Karenne Wood. She prayed in her native language, "welcoming the new arrivals to our land and celebrating the fact that we are still here."

A BRITISH SOLDIER IGNITES a cannon at Fort Frederick, Maryland (opposite) during a French and Indian War reenactment outside Hagerstown near Big Pool. By the time the war began, settlers owned much land but were still pushing the frontier farther west. A British reenactor (below) carefully holds his flintlock musket. Its lock plate is engraved with the year it was produced, 1762.

VITAL WATERWAYS
An aerial view of Fort Frederick near Hagerstown, Maryland, shows its proximity to navigable water: the Chesapeake and Ohio Canal, built in the 1820s, and the parallel Potomac River. The fort was critical to the success of the English during the French and Indian War and later served as a Revolutionary War prison camp.

AN EVER READY MUSKET SITS AT THE entrance to the home of Thomas Cresap at the Chesapeake and Ohio Canal near Fort Frederick. A Maryland frontiersman, Cresap dealt with Indians on the front lines during the French and Indian War.

THREE HUNDRED YEARS AGO, AS THE INDIANS RETREATED from their old homes in the corridor along the Piedmont, their places were taken by energetic and ambitious newcomers. "Manakin Town"—a Monacan town on the James River—was quickly resettled by French Huguenots who had fled persecution in their own country. Moravians fleeing religious persecution in Bohemia and Moravia entered the Monocacy Valley by the middle of the 18th century, as evidenced in the Graceham Church and Parsonage of Frederick County, Maryland. German settlers such as Joseph Bruner, whose home, Schifferstadt (now an architectural museum), still stands in Frederick County, and Scots-Irish settlers moved from

Philadelphia westward into Hallowed Ground territory during the 18th century as well.

Alexander Spotswood, a professional British soldier who arrived in Virginia as lieutenant governor in 1710, contracted with a group of nine families from Germany to occupy a fortified settlement beside a ford on the Rappahannock that was consequently known as Germanna Ford. His aim was to establish an iron mine and iron foundry using the ore he felt sure was in the ground. Three years later he brought in more Germans. Meanwhile the first group, irked by Spotswood's heavy-handed control, struck out on their own, successfully obtaining land grants in what is now Fauquier County, where they established Germantown. Soon after that, the second group also broke free and spread out around the Piedmont to Madison County and Culpeper County. Meanwhile, Spotswood in 1716 had led a group of friends on an expedition to cross the Blue Ridge. They claimed this area for King George I of England, along with all the land to the west as far as the Pacific Ocean.

While populating the Piedmont, where he was also buying up large tracts of land for himself, Spotswood was determined to bring the iron industry to Virginia. By 1720, he had the Tubal ironworks, 13 miles from Germanna, up and running—the first successful ironworks in North America. Within three years he was exporting pig iron to England. (In another first, Tubal marked the initial large-scale use of slaves for industrial work in the country.) This dynamo had accumulated no fewer than 80,000 acres of land and three thriving iron furnaces at the time he was forced out of office by an opponent with better political connections. Today's Route 3 East from Culpeper to Fredericksburg follows a road laid down by Spotswood, as were many other roads in the area. Entire forests disappeared to feed his furnaces.

Among the settlers moving into the frontier zone of the Piedmont were some names that would one day echo around the world. In 1723 Ambrose Madison, a son-in-law of one of the members of Spotswood's westward expedition, took over nearly 5,000 acres not far from the Blue Ridge in what would become Orange County. He moved into a small house on the land with his family and slaves nine years later, only to be poisoned shortly afterward by one of the slaves. His widow, Frances, built up the plantation that would one day pass into the hands of her

A WAR BONNET ON DISPLAY AT James Monroe's estate Ash Lawn-Highland was presented by the Indians to Monroe during his Presidency.

THIS KING GEORGE III SILVER PEACE medal was given by colonial settlers to an Indian to be worn around the neck. When the original hole for hanging wore through, a second one was made below it.

grandson, James Madison, author of the U.S. Constitution. Peter Jefferson, an ambitious, well-connected surveyor and mapmaker, staked his claim to land on Southwest Mountain in 1734, where his son Thomas was born eight years later. In 1749, a precocious 17-year-old surveyor drew up a plan for a new town in the foothills of the Blue Ridge and presented it to his patron, Lord Fairfax, who had been granted five million acres in northern Virginia. Fairfax was so taken with the work that he promptly named the town Washington in honor of its author.

George Washington went on to survey huge acreages of land for Fairfax in the far northwest region of Virginia and in the lands beyond. Firsthand information gained this way put Washington in a good position to invest in land. The pressure of new immigrants from Europe and the need of Tidewater tobacco planters to move to new land because their crop had exhausted the soil of their plantations fueled a speculative land boom across the region. "They rolled forward in waves," explained Kerri Barile, a Fredericksburg archaeologist specializing in the colonial period, "always moving on to fresh land and leaving the depleted soil behind them. In the eastern Piedmont you will often see a field with a grove of trees in the middle. In the trees will be the ruins of a farmhouse, abandoned by the owners."

This pressure for new land led in 1755 to collision with the French colonists pushing down from the Ohio Valley. The French and Indian War represented the struggle over who owned the upper Ohio River Valley and the critical trade paths from the lands of the Hallowed Ground corridor to the rich Midwest. George Washington himself, at 21 years old, provided the spark for what would be the seven-year-long war. Early in April 1754, having received his commission as lieutenant colonel, he led a regiment from Alexandria, Virginia, north and west, intending to build a road through Pennsylvania toward an English fort on the Ohio River. Word reached him at Wills Creek (present-day Cumberland, Maryland) that the fort had been overtaken by the French.

TWIN WINE BOTTLES FROM LUDWELL Park at Norman's Ford date from an early settlement in the Piedmont, around the 1760s. Retrieved from a trench in the cellar, the bottles contained cherry pits, indicating the wine was made from that fruit.

In late May, he and his men camped in a natural clearing called Great Meadows, near what is now Farmingtown, Pennsylvania, 160 miles west of modern day Gettysburg. From there, on the night of May 27, he led three dozen men through the woodland darkness and, aided by Seneca allies, surrounded the fort and surprised the French who camped there. The ensuing conflict resulted in 13 French dead and 21 captured. The survivors were escorted by Washington's troops to imprisonment in Williamsburg, Virginia—a journey of about 330 miles. Washington established a fort at Great Meadows, which he named Fort Necessity. On July 3, he and his men faced an attack by 600 French and 100 Indians. It was Washington's first major military encounter—and his only surrender.

At the beginning of the war that followed, the French were generally victorious. Later, Virginia, Maryland, and other colonial forces, fighting with professional British units, turned the tide. The war ended any French threat to the prosperity and expansion of Virginia, Maryland, Pennsylvania and the neighboring colonies. Now it was time for a young generation, born and raised on the Piedmont frontier, to change the old order and make a new world for themselves.

SALUTING ANCESTRAL SPIRITS
Johnny Rocca, a Tuscarora Indian chief, waves smoke from his peace pipe upward, toward the spirit world and his ancestors. On this battle-field outside Leesburg near the Potomac River, some 12,000 pre-contact Indians died during internecine warfare.

HISTORY REPLAYS ITSELF
Revolutionary War reenactors fire a volley on the grounds of Morven Park
in Leesburg, Virginia. This 1,200-acre-estate of two former governors serves
as the International Equestrian Center, as well as an occasional stage where reenactors preserve history and tradition by educating visitors about the Revolutionary War.

Revolutionary War Era

Revolutionary War Era

One late October day in 1775, a strange-looking army marched into the Tidewater town of Williamsburg, the capital of the Virginia colony. Festooned with tomahawks and scalping knives, these new arrivals in their camouflage shirts represented a raw and dangerous world that the sedate old town had long left behind. "Many people hearing that we were from the backwoods, " one of

them wrote in his diary, "and seeing our dress were as much afraid of us for a few days as if we had been Indians." As the diarist, young Philip Slaughter, recorded, the soldiers' shirts displayed "with large letters the words 'Liberty or Death.'"

JUST SIX MONTHS EARLIER, THE AMERICAN colonists' dispute with Britain had turned bloody at Lexington and Concord in far-off Massachusetts. Now a British army and fleet were threatening the coast of Virginia. The men marching to the rescue were minutemen recruited from the frontier zone of the Piedmont, where they had assembled a month earlier on Philip Clayton's farm near the little town of Culpeper Courthouse. Some, like Slaughter, were from Culpeper County (Clayton was his grandfather). Others had come up from Orange County or down from Fauquier, all linked by the Old Carolina Road, all sons of the land that would come to be known as Hallowed Ground.

In December of that year, these backwoodsmen routed regular British Army troops at the Battle of Great Bridge, near today's Chesapeake,

Virginia, enabling the insurgents to capture the port of Norfolk. Thereafter absorbed into George Washington's Continental Army, many of them fought through the entire war. Abraham Buford, a minuteman colonel, barely survived the "Waxhaw Massacre" in South Carolina, when most of his unit were killed by British troops while surrendering. Slaughter finished the war as a 22-year-old captain, having lived through the freezing winter at Valley Forge, Pennsylvania—one of the few officers who owned enough clothes to accept General Washington's invitations to dinner.

Other patriot soldiers had not been so lucky, shivering and without food or shoes, often leaving trails of blood in the snow from their bare feet. One of those who survived was William Clark, a "free negro" who joined up at the beginning of the war, fought through several major battles, and lived long enough to win his last battle for a veteran's pension, even though he had given his discharge papers for safekeeping to Col. John Jameson, who lost them.

THE RIVANNA RIVER FLOWS NEAR THOMAS JEFFERSON'S MONTICELLO.

THE MINUTEMAN REPRESENTED A NEW KIND OF CITIZEN soldier in the corridor between Gettysburg and Monticello. The coastal Tidewater had been settled a century before by younger sons of the aristocracy from England who lived like feudal lords on their vast plantations. The recruits who joined at Culpeper, on the other hand, came from a land of smaller farms that they or their fathers worked along with just a few slaves living in simple log cabins. Roughly 60 percent of them were literate enough to sign their names. While the struggle had begun as a fight for fair representation in the British Parliament, it evolved into a war for American independence, its ideals crystallized in words recorded by Thomas Jefferson in the 1776 Declaration of Independence.

Not all those living in the Hallowed Ground corridor supported the war, certainly not the Quakers, recently settled in the Colonies—especially Pennsylvania. Their pacifism, born of religious convictions, forbade them from fighting. In Waterford, Virginia, founded by Quakers around 1733, several members of the community nevertheless joined the Continental Army and were summarily expelled from the group. Quakers were also beginning to take a principled stand on slavery. By the late 1700s the Hallowed Ground region held hundreds of free blacks—former slaves or indentured servants, or individuals of biracial parentage who had been born free. Although before 1782 it was illegal to free a slave in Virginia, Quaker planters were doing so to an increasing extent by the time the Revolutionary War broke out in 1776. By 1800 there were 20,000 free blacks in Virginia, to its 290,000 slaves.

Others of these new citizen soldiers were small-business owners, self-made entrepreneurs like John Jouette. Jouette raised four sons in Albemarle County, Virginia, one of whom died fighting in the 1777 Battle of Brandywine in Pennsylvania. One of Jouette's other sons, Jack, was to play an even more important role in the war, in an arguably more dramatic manner. Great Bridge was a gateway to upland Virginia, an American stronghold whose protection was seen as critical. Headquarters to patriot leaders such as Gen. Anthony Wayne, Gilbert du Motier de Lafayette, and John Mühlenberg, it was also home to Founding Fathers Thomas Jefferson, James Madison, and James Monroe, all young visionaries at the time, destined all to become Presidents who shaped a new nation. The British mounted an abortive raid on Monticello and Charlottesville meant to capture Thomas Jefferson, then governor of Virginia, who was meeting with his legislature. The contingent included future Presidents John Tyler and Benjamin Harrison, as well as Patrick Henry, Richard Henry Lee, and Daniel Boone. The plan failed, thanks to the courage and daring of Jack Jouette. Jouette, later called the Paul Revere of the South, raced by horseback across 40 miles of treacherous terrain to warn a sleeping Jefferson of the danger.

In the harsh winter of 1777, Hessian mercenaries on contract to the British, who had surrendered with Gen. John Burgoyne at Saratoga, New York, were brought south across the Potomac into Virginia and marched to a camp in Charlottesville. Although many in the Piedmont were vehement in their hatred for any representative of the British crown, General Washington resolved to treat the Hessian prisoners civilly, and as a result, 900 prisoners from the Battle of Trenton marched unescorted from Maryland to Virginia. Treated humanely at the prison camps (often farms along

FOR THE PAST 45 YEARS AN AUDIENCE has gathered at Monticello on July Fourth to observe a U.S. citizenship ceremony. Every year, the 75 individuals randomly scheduled to receive their citizenship on that day may choose to take their oath at Jefferson's neoclassic masterpiece. The guest speaker in 2007 was actor Sam Waterston, whose father came to this country as a Scottish immigrant.

A HAVEN FOR THE LIFE OF THE MIND
Jefferson's private suite at Monticello reveals his ardent pursuit
of intellectual topics and his patriotism, as well as his inventive bent.
Busts of John Adams and George Washington overlook the room.

the Piedmont) in which they were housed, many chose to settle in the area at the war's end.

BACK ON THAT FALL DAY IN CULPEPER WHEN IT ALL BEGAN, Philip Slaughter took note of one of his fellow recruits at Clayton's field, decked out in a pale blue hunting shirt and trousers, fringed with white. The dandy was the future Chief Justice of the United States, 19-year-old John Marshall from Fauquier.

While Marshall began drilling fellow recruits—he was quickly promoted to lieutenant—20 miles down the road another young man, 24-year-old James Madison, a colonel in the Orange County militia, was also training troops. Thomas Jefferson was in Philadelphia as a member of the Continental Congress, vehement in his support for a total break from Britain. James Monroe was a law student at the College of William and Mary, busily organizing an insurgent military unit on campus. A year later, already a colonel at the age of 18, he would be crossing the Delaware River in George Washington's army. Washington himself, whose first public job had been surveyor of Culpeper County and who owned thousands of acres in the region, was outside Boston, commanding a ragtag

POLYGRAPH ON JEFFERSON'S DESK (below) made duplicate copies of his correspondence. As he wrote with one pen, an additional pen, attached to it by rigid pieces of wood, wrote simultaneously. He replaced the device with a succession of improved ones, some with as many as five pens, but always used the two-pen model.

army woefully short of men and supplies and facing the most powerful empire on Earth.

This was the true "Greatest Generation," all of whom either came from or spent the best part of their lives here in the Virginia Piedmont. Why here? Partly it was a matter of timing. A hundred years earlier, their families had all been back in the Tidewater. If the American Revolution had broken out 50 years later, the best and the brightest would have been elsewhere. "It's a snapshot of where a particular generation resided," said Daniel P. Jordan, president of the Thomas Jefferson Foundation. "Take another snapshot from 1850. By then, 388,000 native-born Virginians had left the state to go elsewhere. They had moved west, or southwest, so if the Revolution had occurred then, you wouldn't have had that same constellation in the Piedmont."

This was a society with few degrees of separation. Marshall grew up in a four-room cabin close under the Blue Ridge that he shared with 11 other members of his family, and he went to school with James Monroe. He was recruited for the minutemen by his father, who in turn was inspired to join by hearing the famous "Give me liberty or give me death" speech by the firebrand attorney Patrick Henry. Henry was Jefferson's close friend at that time and the first cousin of Madison's future wife, Dolley. John Marshall eventually married Mary Ambler, the daughter of Rebecca Burwell, whom a tongue-tied Jefferson had courted with ineffective passion at the age of 20. James Monroe sold his farm—located in the middle of the property that was eventually turned into Jefferson's University of Virginia—to move closer to his friend at Monticello.

These were all strong-willed, independent-minded men and women, with widely divergent ideas about the kind of country they were or should be creating. Although they lived on the edge of civilization, their expressed ideals would help to define civilized society for centuries to come. Washington, resolute even in the darkest times, led the Colonies to victory before emerging from retirement to serve as the newborn nation's first President. Jefferson and Marshall debated passionately on the role of the central government and judiciary, yet they both pursued visions

AN ORIGINAL COPY OF JEFFERSON'S "Notes on the State of Virginia" reveals not only his impressive knowledge of the area's land and people, but also his expertise concerning agriculture and industry. It also reflects his views on the current and future state of the new nation, the latter a declaration of hope interspersed with anxiety.

THOMAS JEFFERSON
Dappled early morning sunlight falls across the wise visage of Thomas
Jefferson, hanging in portraiture in the main foyer of his home at Monticello.
The signature painting was created from life by Thomas Sully in 1821.

DAN JORDAN

**MAKE NO MISTAKE ABOUT IT, OUR HERTIAGE IS VERY MUCH IN DANGER.
UNINFORMED DEVELOPMENT AND SPRAWL CAN AND WILL DEPRIVE
FUTURE GENERATIONS OF THIS NATIONAL TREASURE.**

Dan Jordan has been president since 1985 of the Thomas Jefferson Foundation, which owns and operates Jefferson's extraordinary Monticello, just outside Charolttesville, Virginia.

"The Journey Through Hallowed Ground reflects a stewardship of place as well as ideas that is unequaled anywhere else in America. To go from Monticello to Gettysburg is to cover two consequential chapters in our nation's history. In between, amazingly, all other eras are reflected: from a very rich Native American culture, step by step, down to the 21st century. The journey traverses pristine areas that must be preserved, if only for what they tell us about our nation's core values, because it would be difficult to think of a consequential American value that is not reflected in the past of this one small area. Think of future generations, and what has to be saved for their edification and inspiration. The journey tells an inclusive story—Native Americans, enslaved African Americans, tens of thousands of young boys fighting on two sides of the

Dan Jordan, president,
Thomas Jefferson Foundation

greatest internal event in our history. And so it goes. There are heroes and villains, and we can learn from all of them, but only if we have the courage and the vision to protect this majestic corridor for the future. This is why it is so important to disclose this heritage that is not only vital to our nation, but also at risk. Make no mistake about it, our heritage is very much in danger. Uninformed development and sprawl can and will deprive future generations of this national treasure.

"Monticello in itself also represents a stewardship of place and ideas. Our mission is preservation and education. We're here to save and to share. The stakes are very high, because Monticello is the only home in America on the World Heritage List and enjoys an iconic status around the globe. Furthermore, the ideas of Thomas Jefferson have never been more important than today. He first wrote what we now all believe, articulating better than anyone our core beliefs in democracy and freedom. It is important to keep him in perspective—as one African American jurist wrote, 'He was imperfect. We all are. But he had some perfect ideas.'"

for a nation of liberty. Jefferson, who would become the third
President, wrote the Declaration of Independence and championed
individual freedom throughout his life. Marshall, who would be
known as the United States' most influential Chief Justice, crafted
the role of the Judiciary as a third pillar of American government. In
addition to these two statesmen, Madison, the Constitution's chief
architect, would serve as the nation's fourth President, and would
negotiate with Jefferson, Alexander Hamilton, and Pennsylvanian
lawmakers the location of the nation's capital between Maryland
and Virginia. Monroe, as the fifth President, would author the
Monroe Doctrine, the landmark foreign policy statement that
warned European powers against colonizing the Americas. George
Mason would father the Bill of Rights. Most, with the exception of
George Washington, were highly educated, with a deep grounding
in the language and history of the ancient Roman Republic and
Athenian democracy. Jefferson, Monroe, and Marshall all attended

the College of William and Mary, which had recently been reorganized under the inspiration of the Scottish Enlightenment, a wellspring of creativity in every area from political science to geology. Jefferson's "self-evident" truths and "pursuit of happiness" in the Declaration of Independence were tributes to Plato's *Republic* and early papal encyclicals and were informed by Scottish philosophers. James Madison had been absorbing his own brand of learning with similar derivatives at

Princeton. These were among the finest minds in the world at the time, each, by fortunate circumstance, living within the region—proximate enough to have both a meeting of ideas and a healthy debate on their intentions.

SUZIE BLANCHARD, CO-OWNER OF the Inn at Meander Plantation and professional chef, gives cooking lessons to guests at the inn during a gourmet cooking weekend. The property has been a working plantation throughout its history.

Others in the area joined these Virginia leaders in establishing the ideals for the new nation, most notably John Hanson of Frederick, Maryland. A scholar of political philosophy and a brilliant leader in the Maryland Assembly, Hanson and his extended family played a range of roles in the fight for independence. As Maryland delegate to the Continental Congress from 1780 to 1782, he helped draft the Articles of Confederation. With their adoption in 1781, the new nation was formed and Congress, including George Washington, elected Hanson the first President. Although the term was limited to one year, Hanson has been praised as a strong and diplomatic leader. He and the six other one-term Presidents helped transition the nation from war into peacetime, preparing the way for the Constitution and George Washington's election in 1789.

All of these men had faults, of course. Their uncomplaining ownership of slaves (even if they sometimes lamented the existence of slavery as an institution) looms as a permanent blot on their records. Jefferson, in particular, stands out for professing a belief in democracy while owning more than a hundred slaves. These men and women shaped Monticello's wood, metal, wool, and linen into useful and beautiful objects and worked agricultural feats. The multitalented Wormley Hughes, a top producer in Jefferson's nailery, was also the stable manager and the gardener for Monticello's breathtaking ornamental lawns.

Yet Jefferson's uncompromising statement in the Declaration of Independence, "All men are created equal," was to become a universal

ROSE HILL MANOR
A blacksmith shows a forged ornament to a visitor at Rose Hill Manor, former home of Thomas Johnson, first elected governor of Maryland and good friend of George Washington. Rose Hill Manor is now operated by the state of Maryland as a children's museum.

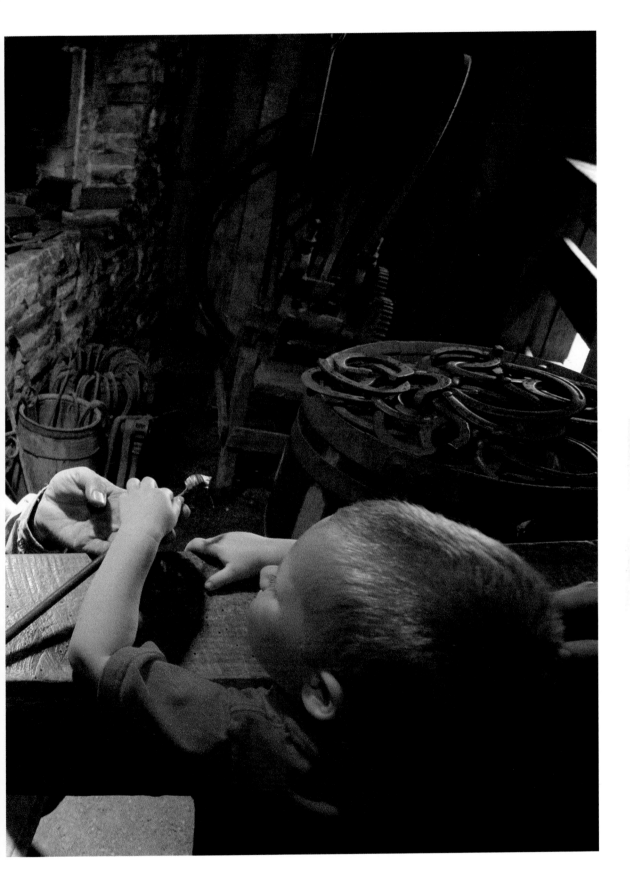

A ONCE ACTIVE IRON-PRODUCING complex, Catoctin Furnace, at Cunningham Falls State Park near Thurmont, Maryland, is a testament to the region's earliest endeavors to create an industrial revolution. Here, Thomas Johnson produced iron for munitions for the Continental Army.

truth. Those "inalienable rights" that he slipped into the Declaration as a fundamental national principle inexorably expanded over the next two centuries to include slaves, women, and other previously excluded Americans. John Charles Thomas, the first African American to sit on the Supreme Court of Virginia, summed up the contradiction best when he told an audience at Monticello, "Jefferson was imperfect. We all are. But he had some perfect ideas."

HOWEVER MUCH JEFFERSON AND HIS FRIENDS STAYED IN touch with the latest European intellectual and artistic fashions, they still existed close to the rim of what was considered the civilized world, on land transformed within living memory from a harsh wilderness. Decades later, a former slave at Monticello remembered "wolves so plenty that they had to build pens round black people's quarters and pen sheep in 'em to keep the wolves from catching them. ...When the snow was on the groun', you could see the wolves in gangs runnin' and howlin.'"

At least the Piedmont had been mapped—most successfully by Jefferson's father, Peter. Far to the west, beyond today's Pennsylvania and West Virginia, there was the golden promise of limitless territory, even if no one was sure what kinds of animals besides wolves might be roaming on the far side of the Mississippi. George Washington had long been convinced that America's destiny lay to the west. "There is a large Field before you," he wrote in 1767 to a friend who had gone broke in the tobacco business and was appealing to him for another loan, "an opening prospect in the back Country for Adventurers … where an enterprising Man with very little Money may lay the foundation of a Noble Estate." But even the noblest estate in the back country needed some way of reaching the outside world, and that was where the rivers flowing across the territory came into play. In Washington's view, the highway clearly had to be the Potomac River, which flowed past his Mount Vernon estate from deep in the interior, where he happened to own vast tracts of land. "The navigation of this river," he declared grandly, "is equal, if not superior to any in the Union … this will become the great avenue into the Western Country."

ROSE HILL MANOR IN FREDERICK, Maryland, was the final home of Thomas Johnson, the first proprietor of Catoctin Furnace and first governor of Maryland. Today, in addition to housing a children's museum, the manor incorporates a park and garden open to the public.

A CONFLUENCE OF RIVERS
An aerial view of Harpers Ferry, West Virginia, where the Shenandoah River (left) and the Potomac River (right) merge into one single Potomac. George Washington chose to build the United States Armory and Arsenal here.

HESSIAN BARRACKS STILL STAND
in the center of Frederick, Maryland. The Hessians, Germans hired to fight with the British, were imprisoned 40 to a room in these barracks after their capture of Saratoga. Prison life here was far from difficult; while they continued to collect salaries from the British, they were also allowed to work the local farms around Frederick and receive compensation for their labor. After the war, many of them remained in the country and integrated into American society. Some of these soldiers were marched south into Virginia, where they were also eventually absorbed into society. During the Civil War the two buildings were again used as prisoner barracks. Later, they became the foundation for the Maryland School for the Deaf, still in operation today.

In 1785 Washington's newly formed Patowmack Company set to work on the first stage of opening up the river, from Great Falls, Virginia, all the way to Harpers Ferry, in West Virginia, where the river, joined by the Shenandoah, bursts through the Blue Ridge. The remains of canals and locks hewn out of solid rock by Washington's company to take boats around falls and rapids can still be seen on the Virginia side of the Potomac. This territory, so recently on the outer rim of civilization, was becoming a bridge to the new frontier.

Unlike Washington, an intrepid frontiersman who marched and canoed across thousands of miles of unmapped wilderness in his time, Jefferson never traveled farther west than the Shenandoah. But his imagination, anchored in vast reading and unquenchable curiosity, soared over the mountains and beyond. More than any of the other Founding Fathers he conceived of the United States as a continental power, stretching from sea to sea. So, although deeply wary of letting the federal government assume excessive power, he had no hesitation as President in snapping up the Louisiana Territory in 1803 when Napoleon put it up for sale, thereby doubling the size of the United States overnight. When it came time

MODERN-DAY CANALMEN guide a replica of an 18th-century boat through Virginia's Seneca Bypass, the only remaining water-filled portion of George Washington's Patowmack Canal. He conceived a series of locks above Great Falls on the Potomac River that, when built, connected traders with the West. This gave them an alternative to the northern routes, which led them to British competitors via the Great Lakes, and the Mississippi route, which led to the Spanish. The waterway system was in operation from 1788 to 1830, when the Chesapeake and Ohio Canal on the Maryland side of the river opened a company and the old Patowmack canal system fell into disrepair. But Washington had instigated this progressive idea, which allowed trade to expand in the early days of the country. More important, the problems of interstate commerce that arose from travel on Washington's Patowmack Canal led to discussions toward unifying the Colonies. With time, these discussions became the foundation for creating the U.S. Constitution and moving the loosely affiliated independent Colonies into a new nation.

Here, a medal signifying membership in the Society of the Cincinnati hangs from a light-blue and white ribbon. It consists of a bald eagle surrounding a medallion that depicts the Roman consul Cincinnatus, who served his country in a wartime emergency. Original members were American and French military participants in the American Revolution. George Washington served as the society's first president general. To the right of the medal is an early portrait of the general. Washington, wearing full military regalia, sits in profile against a rich blue background.

to assign an explorer to travel west, Jefferson felt no need to look further than Meriwether Lewis, a Virginian who not only was his secretary but also his neighbor, raised just a few miles from Monticello. A man of "undaunted courage," Jefferson later wrote, Lewis, with co-captain William Clark and their small Corps of Discovery, forged the first path from the Hallowed Ground region all the way to the Pacific Ocean and back, from 1803 to 1806, and made America aware of its vast holdings beyond the Blue Ridge. America was moving west. Meanwhile, there was much to be done on the home farm.

AS FARMERS, THESE FOUNDING FATHERS HAD TO HAVE A deep awareness of everything to do with the land—soils, planting and harvesting times, crop rotation, weather, blights, irrigation, and pests, all of which they could discuss in great technical detail. Gardeners today can admire the clever ideas Jefferson designed into the artfully positioned thousand-foot-long vegetable garden, situated down

the slope from the kitchens at Monticello. He could not have kept this garden productive without slaves like Wormley Hughes, whose expert gardening was cited often in Jefferson's journals. Jefferson's meticulously kept farm books are full of the most detailed records and plans for the management of his plantation, even if he was likely to be distracted from the more routine aspects of farming. (Meanwhile, James Monroe—who bought the farm next door to Monticello—was, according to a neighboring farmer, "an indifferent manager … nearly always in debt.") James Madison was also deeply involved in farming his plantation at Montpelier. More patient than Jefferson, the master builder of the U.S. Constitution earnestly studied all the most up-to-date notions about crop rotation and contour plowing. Most notably, he could claim to be the first Virginia conservationist. Thanks to him, some of the original forest at Montpelier has survived.

Unfortunately, the accelerating disappearance of the Piedmont's woodland had a lot to do with efforts by planters like Madison,

THIS BRONZE STATUE OF JAMES Madison, who is often referred to as the architect of the U.S. Constitution, rests in front of a copy of the Constitution at Montpelier. It is three-quarters the size of the original statue, which honors the country's fourth President in the James Madison Memorial Library at the Library of Congress.

Jefferson, and Washington to escape the crop that had made their families rich in the first place. Like Monticello, Montpelier had been established as a plantation for tobacco, a crop that so dominated Virginia in the mid-18th century that it was legal tender. Peter Jefferson and Ambrose Madison had carved out their estates when the soil was still fertile, not worn out by decades of tobacco production like the soil of the Tidewater. In the 1760s, tobacco prices had started to decline, which meant that the London merchants were no longer quite so happy to loan money for fancy furniture, fine coaches, extra slaves, and other necessities of a planter's life. Even worse, when the debts remained unpaid the coldhearted English businessmen had little compunction in forcing the debtors into bankruptcy. To some, such as Thomas Jefferson and George Washington, this situation amounted to nothing less than a deliberate assault on liberty. "It is but an irksome thing for a *free mind* to be always hampered in Debt," Washington told a London merchant who was pressing him for repayment in 1764.

THOMAS JEFFERSON WAS AN EXPERT ON A GREAT MANY subjects. He was, after all, the only President also to have been president of the American Philosophical Society (the leading scientific body of the day). The thousands of documents in his hand that survive, many duplicated by the copying device he perfected, are a testament to his curiosity and expertise, as well as a road map to his life and works. But there are gaps in the paper trail, most notoriously in the case of his relationship with Sally Hemings, the slave fathered by John Wayles, who was also the father of Jefferson's wife, Martha. The true nature of the Jefferson-Hemings relationship was long a subject of debate and controversy. However, following a DNA study in 1998, scholars confirmed that the two produced at least one child, Eston Hemings. Much about the lives of the slaves who served Jefferson and others like him is coming to light today. Monticello has an extensive African-American oral history project, "Getting Word." From it we know that Isaac Jefferson, the only slave ever to hold the position of overseer at Monticello, was both a leader and a gifted tinsmith and that the "half Virginian, half French" cuisine of Edith Fossett was applauded by statesman Daniel Webster. And there is another kind of record, buried under the soil of the Monticello Mountain and rendered legible today by archaeologists' patient detective work.

Although Monticello survives in the state that Jefferson conceived it, the log cabins inhabited by the slaves who made all this possible

A BRONZE BUST OF JAMES MONROE, sculpted by Attilio Piccirilli in 1931, sits on a drop leaf table in the entrance hall of Ash Lawn-Highland, his small first home, purchased in 1793. This shaper of the Monroe Doctrine could view neighboring Monticello from his own door.

have long gone; still, subtle traces of the people who lived there survive, and their stories resonate today. Under the brow of the mountain, running almost to the Rivanna River, which curls around the estate, is the "Ancient Field," a 60-acre tract planted with tobacco by Jefferson's father back in the 1740s. "Tobacco was a gang labor operation," explained Fraser D. Neiman, chief archaeologist at the Thomas Jefferson Foundation, as we walked through the woods that now cover Jefferson's field. "Essentially you had a group all doing the same thing." With the gang all in one place, it could be watched by a single overseer. These gangs lived close by the fields they worked, crowded into cramped barracks. "Each one would have housed four families," said Neiman.

There is no sign on the wooded slope today that dozens of people once lived and worked there. But Neiman and his team have learned much about how they lived. Slaves on the Virginia tobacco plantations developed the custom of digging little storage pits under

SOMERSET PLANTATION NEAR

Montpelier fronts a scenic view of Virginia's Blue Ridge mountains much as Madison himself would have witnessed in the early days of the nation.

"JEFFERSON WAS
IMPERFECT, WE
ALL ARE. BUT
HE HAD SOME
PERFECT IDEAS."

*—John Charles
Thomas, the first
African American to
sit on the Supreme
Court of Virginia*

A BRONZE LIFE-SIZE STATUE OF
John Marshall, Chief Justice of the United
States from 1801 to 1835, sits outside
the courthouse in Warrenton, Virginia
(below). His home (right), now privately
owned, lies two miles west of Marshall,
Virginia. Marshall's legacy was to strengthen
the judicial branch of government.

their crowded barracks to store personal possessions, precious items such as buttons and, most of all, ceramics—plates and cups. Though many plowing seasons have torn up these hiding places, broken sherds and fragments unearthed and ingeniously analyzed from archaeological digs have revealed a previously unknown story of what happened when Jefferson decided to free himself from the "wretchedness" of tobacco.

Throwing off British rule was one way of escaping the debt trap of the tobacco system—following the Revolution, most of the planters' British debts were never paid. But planters also began shifting to a different crop that would allow them a fresh start— wheat. Wrote Jefferson in 1782, "It feeds the labourers plentifully, requires from them only a moderate toil, except in the season of harvest, raises great numbers of animals for food and service, and diffuses plenty and happiness...." He also invented a new kind of plow. In 1794, after retiring as secretary of state in the Washington Administration, he started planting the new crop, with far-reaching consequences for the land and those who worked it.

Tobacco could be planted in patches between tree stumps, or slave dwellings, or on hillsides. The patches were regularly moved,

THE IMPORTANCE OF WHEAT GROWING
Ivan Lufriu, miller at Union Mills, grinds corn in the still operating facility, now more than 200 years old. Mills like this one were not only places of employment and industry for early Americans, but also centers of social interaction and information. Now a living history museum, it represents wheat's importance in the Westminster-Gettysburg area.

leaving the soil to regenerate itself before it was replanted a few years later. Sowing wheat, on the other hand, required lots of uninterrupted open space, which meant that the land had to be cleared of everything, including trees. This proved disastrous for any sloping land like the Ancient Field spread across the Monticello Mountain. Denuded of trees, the topsoil rapidly eroded downhill, propeled by summer downpours. Meanwhile, any slave dwellings were swept away along with the trees. There is no mention of this change in Jefferson's meticulously kept farm books, but the archaeologists' detective work has revealed that the large barracks housing multiple slave families disappeared at the same time Jefferson planted wheat.

Just at this time, a new kind of slave cabin appeared. These were smaller, each inhabited by only one family. What had happened? Neiman thinks he has the answer. Wheat was altogether a more complicated operation, requiring plows, animals to pull the plows, forage crops for the animals to eat, manure for fertilization, carts to move the manure, and drivers for the plows and carts. "That meant you had a lot of slaves doing different things in different places at the same time," he explained, "and you couldn't have an overseer for each one." If the slaves had to do their work without any overseer present to punish them if they idled, perhaps they were now being offered a little incentive, such as the right to live on their own as a family unit.

Among the scattered sherds of glass and pottery left behind by the occupants of one cabin, the archaeologists found clues to a slave's surreptitious efforts to make his life a little better at Jefferson's expense—fragments of metal rods used for making nails. Around 1800, Jefferson had started importing nail rods from foundries in Philadelphia for the nail factory he had set up below the kitchen yard at the top of the hill. Clearly, someone was taking some of Jefferson's metal to make nails on his own account. There is no record of who lived in this cabin, but the rods call to mind a slave named Jamey Hubbard. A nephew of Sally Hemings's nephew, Hubbard was raised on another Jefferson plantation and brought to Monticello to labor in the nail factory at the age of 11. In 1796, when he was 13, Hubbard made a record seven pounds of eight-penny nails in one day, which meant he swung his hammer more than 20,000 times. At age 21, he escaped, carrying forged papers, but was quickly caught and returned. At 27, Hubbard ran away again. This time he stayed free for a year before being caught, returned to Monticello, and flogged. Jefferson had already sold him, and advised the buyer to sell him again, out of state, because he "will never again serve any man as a slave." What happened next we will probably never know, because no further record of Jamey Hubbard has survived.

THE GAP BETWEEN THE RICH WHITE PLANTER AND THE flogged slave, even if he happened to be cousin to the planter's own children, was light-years wide. Thanks to the complicated legal distortions of slavery, matters were slightly different if the father was a slave and the mother free, in which case the children were also free. Such was the case with Sarah Madden, born in 1758. Her

A STATUE OF FRANCIS SCOTT KEY appropriately displays the author of "The Star-Spangled Banner" with one hand upheld and the other outstretched toward an American flag flying in the cemetery where he is buried, outside Frederick, Maryland. Born nearby at Terra Rubra, he grew up in the area and graduated from St. John's College in Annapolis. The circumstances that were to bring him lasting fame as creator of America's premier hymn to patriotism occurred during the War of 1812 in Baltimore Harbor, on September 13-14, 1814. Throughout that day and during the night he watched as the battle raged against the British. With the coming of dawn, Key saw at last what he had been hoping to see: the huge American flag flying majestically over Fort McHenry, signifying the nation's victory.

FREEDMAN'S CABIN
The humble kitchen of a log cabin built by a former slave born on James Madison's property in 1810 still stands in its restored condition today. After the Civil War he received 16 acres across the road from Montpelier to begin his free life.

REBECCA GILMORE COLEMAN

IT'S SO IMPORTANT THAT PEOPLE TALK ABOUT THEIR FAMILY STORIES,
BECAUSE TO KNOW WHERE YOU'RE GOING,
YOU MUST KNOW WHERE YOU HAVE BEEN.

Rebecca Gilmore Coleman, president of the Orange County African American Historical Association, is involved in tracing the record of her family and its connections to James Madison's Montpelier. She donated the Gilmore cabin and its land to Montpelier and has been active in its restoration for educational purposes.

"My great-grandfather, George Coleman, was born around 1810 as a slave on the Montpelier plantation, which at that time belonged to President James Madison.... George was born around 1810, according to the census records, which was so often the only family history information from those days that existed for African Americans. Unfortunately most of the slave records of President Madison were burned ... which created a big problem for my family, and other African American families like ours, whose histories were recorded (with just a first name in many cases) only by the slave-owners. We're still searching the archives to find out more about our ancestors. From the census records and other documents we do know that George was a farmer, a carpenter, a beekeeper. Clearly, he was able to use the skills he learned as a slave to provide for his family. This information came from tax records. He was freed by emancipation, and later he built a cabin on the 16 acres he was able to purchase from Dr. Ambrose Madison, the great nephew of President Madison. He built the cabin in 1873. My grandfather Philip was born in that cabin, and so was my father. In 1901 George was able to buy the land, for $560. He died in 1905.

"I grew up six miles from Montpelier, but I didn't know any of this story until the 1970s, when my father took me to the cabin and told me about his Grandfather George and the Madisons. I wish I had started looking into the family history before so many people who could have helped me had passed. So much has been lost. African Americans have very little to say about their past. Hopefully more of us will want to learn as much as we can about our family histories. It's so important that people talk about their family stories, because to know where you're going, you must know where you have been."

Rebecca Gilmore Coleman,
preservationist and educator

mother was Mary Madden, a poor Irish immigrant. Sarah's father was said to be a slave on the plantation of Col. James Madison, Sr., father of the architect of the Constitution. Because Mary was not a slave, her biracial child was free. On the other hand, having a child with a black person was against the law, punishable by a heavy fine, which Mary could not pay, so she was indentured—essentially sold as a temporary slave for a number of years in lieu of the money. As she could not support her baby, Sarah was taken away and herself indentured, ending up on the Madison plantation, but she eventually managed to regain her freedom and earn a living doing laundry and sewing.

Sarah died in 1824, but her energy and resourcefulness were inherited by her son Willis, who married Kitty Clark, the daughter of William Clark, the black soldier who had fought in Washington's army 50 years before. Despite the enormous obstacles carefully placed in the path of any ambitious black man—not allowed to vote, not allowed to sell liquor, not allowed to marry legally (Kitty was a common-law wife), not allowed to own a weapon, not educated, officially not even allowed to live in Virginia—Willis managed to buy land and, ultimately, open a tavern near Culpeper where the Old Carolina Road crossed the road from the western Piedmont down to Fredericksburg. By the 1840s Madden's Tavern had become the most successful and prosperous in the whole area.

Both Madden and Jefferson left monuments in the Hallowed Ground. The tavern still stands as a testament to its builder's ingenuity and perseverance. Monticello provides evidence of Jefferson's quirks (he once cut holes in the floor for a wall clock's weights), artistic skill, and ingenuity. In fact, the carefully tended Monticello today better conveys Jefferson's architectural vision than it ever did in his lifetime, since he was continually altering and rebuilding. The same might be said of his ideas, uttered in a time when few accepted that all men really were created equal, still less universally entitled to the pursuit of happiness. Today, just as Monticello stands complete, looking out over a view little changed since his time, so Jefferson's ideas are accepted by people the world over.

He and his colleagues, hailing from a radius of scarcely more than a hundred miles, together had laid the founding ideals for a nation that would span 3,000 miles from sea to sea and would endure for centuries. Jefferson was long buried in the cemetery at Monticello when these ideals were put to a terrible test. The story of how they endured that trial is a testament to their vitality.

"THE NAVIGATION OF THIS RIVER IS EQUAL, IF NOT SUPERIOR TO ANY IN THE UNION . . . THIS WILL BECOME THE GREAT AVENUE INTO THE WESTERN COUNTRY."

—*George Washington on the Potomac River*

THE ROTUNDA
The Rotunda glows in the snow on the Lawn at the University of Virginia, also known as Mr. Jefferson's University. Thomas Jefferson, inspired by the Pantheon in Rome, designed the building to represent "the authority of nature and power of reason."

CHAPTER THREE

Civil War Times

STEADFAST SOLDIER
A Union soldier reenactor stands by an 1864 U.S. flag at Gettysburg's Lincoln Cemetery on Remembrance Day. A special ceremony is held for black soldiers, who continue to be buried there.

Civil War Times

"I MUST SIDE EITHER WITH OR AGAINST MY SECTION ... I CANNOT RAISE MY HAND AGAINST MY BIRTHPLACE, MY HOME, MY CHILDREN."
—ROBERT E. LEE, OPPONENT OF SLAVERY, WHO SERVED AS CONFEDERATE COMMANDER

On June 29, 1861, two months after southern secessionists fired on Fort Sumter and launched the Civil War, President Abraham Lincoln called his senior military advisers to the White House for a strategy meeting. Lincoln and his advisers were evaluating plans to crush the rebellion. The general commanding the army proposed a plan to strangle the Confederacy by blockading its coasts and

seizing control of the Mississippi, thus suffocating the Rebel economy and restoring the Union with little bloodshed. But for many in the North, this was too patient and cautious an approach. Richmond, the Rebel capital, after all, was only a four-day march from Washington. "Forward to Richmond!" cried the northern press, eager for a quick victory. At the White House, therefore, Quartermaster Gen. Montgomery Meigs argued that "it was better to whip them here than to go far into an unhealthy country to fight them [on the Mississippi].... To make the fight in Virginia was cheaper and better."

Lincoln agreed, and the die was cast. The land that had contributed so much to the birth of the Republic would now host a pitiless struggle for its future. Close to Washington, in full view of the nation's and the world's press, the land between the falls and the mountains would serve as a bloody arena for young men to fight to the death.

IT WAS AS IF NATURE HAD DESIGNED THE area to be a battlefield. Thanks to ancient geologic events, the warring armies would be channeled on one side by the falls and on the other by the Blue Ridge Mountains. Between them the landscape extended in form into southwestern Maryland and southern Pennsylvania, broken occasionally by other mountains, such as Bull Run, that were useful for screening the movement of troops. Just as the fords on the rivers had marked the route for Indian hunting parties and Thomas Jefferson's journeys to and from Philadelphia, they now guided Union and Confederate forces north and south. Most of the Piedmont terrain with its gentle hills, open farmland, and woods offered no great obstacles to moving troops or fighting battles, and the fields and pastures supplied rations for passing armies and grass for their horses. The only major change since Jefferson's time was the network of railroads, supply lines vital to the Confederacy, in the case of the Orange and Alexandria line, or to the Union, such as the Baltimore and Ohio, which connected Washington to the West. Railroads let armies stay in the field longer than before, assured of constant supplies of ammunition, and of necessities like newspapers and mail.

THIS STONE HOUSE IN MANASSAS, VIRGINIA, WAS BUILT IN 1848.

GEN. THOMAS JACKSON SITS
astride his mount on a statue commemorating him at Manassas National Battlefield Park, where at the First Battle of Bull Run he earned the nickname Stonewall. After Robert E. Lee, he was the most revered Confederate general, but his brilliant career was cut short when he was mortally wounded at the Battle of Chancellorsville in May 1863.

Despite being the choice of leaders on both sides as the ideal ground for deciding the issues of slavery and states' rights that had torn the nation apart, residents were not at all sure that they wanted the honor. Virginians actually initially voted to remain in the Union. Only a third of the Virginia state legislature at the beginning of 1861 was in favor of leaving the Union, and those members were from the conservative east and south of the state. In the northwest, where few people owned slaves, the mood ran quite the other way, leading to the creation of West Virginia. Even so, the prologue to the drama of the war was enacted in the then Virginian town of Harpers Ferry, where John Brown, the militant abolitionist, had seized the federal armory in 1859 with the hope of sparking a general slave uprising. Though his methods were strident and ultimately cost him his life, he doggedly pursued the American ideal of equality. Virginia eventually joined the cotton states only after Lincoln's call for troops.

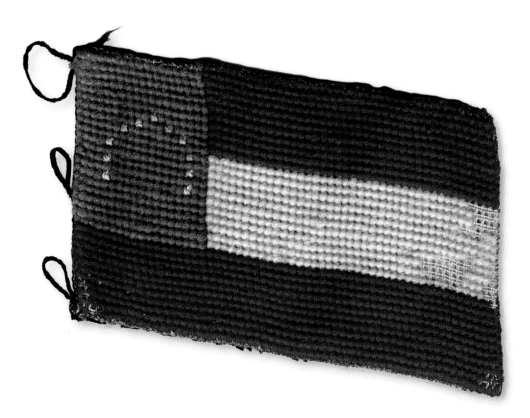

Those for whom he struggled were slaves such as Catherine "Kitty" Payne. In 1843, Payne was freed by her Virginian owner, Mary Maddox, who escorted her and her four small children to Adams County, Pennsylvania. However, Maddox's nephew, Samuel Maddox, decided to "claim" what he saw as his inheritance. He kidnapped Payne and her children in Pennsylvania, spiriting them back to Rappahannock County, Virginia. His plan to sell Payne and her children fell through when Payne somehow managed to sue him; still, Rappahannock County imprisoned the family for more than a year. Eventually the public outrage and support from Quakers in Adams County and Loudoun County helped free them.

For such injustice John Brown gave his life at Harpers Ferry. And here, in 1906, civil rights activist and writer W. E. B. Du Bois convened a meeting that launched the Niagara Movement, which inspired Mary White Ovington to co-found the National Association for the Advancement of Colored People (NAACP).

Ironically, the army officer who put an end to John Brown's demonstration was an opponent of slavery, calling it "a moral and political evil." He also opposed the secession of Virginia from the Union that his father, a Revolutionary War hero, had fought to create. He was even offered command of the Union armies. But

MARY CUSTIS LEE, THE WIFE OF Robert E. Lee, presented this "housewife," or sewing kit, to John Singleton Mosby as a token of her appreciation for his work on behalf of the southern cause. She needlepointed it with the headquarters' flag motif containing 13 stars (only 11 remain). Its satin-lined interior contains needles, thread, and buttons. She presented many such gifts to favorite officers serving under her husband.

THE BLOODIEST DAY OF THE CIVIL WAR
In an aerial view of Bloody Lane, or Sunken Road, at Antietam Battlefield, split rail fences mark the area where some 23,000 troops from both sides became casualties in Lee's first foray into Union territory in 1862.

when Virginia voted to secede, Robert E. Lee declared, "I must side either with or against my section … I cannot raise my hand against my birthplace, my home, my children." A Confederate soldier captured in Virginia early on put it more succinctly. Asked why he, a non-slaveholder, was fighting to defend slavery, he told his captors, "I'm fighting because you're down here."

MOST OF THE LAND THAT HAD PRODUCED JEFFERSON, Madison, Monroe, and Marshall supported the Confederacy. Col. Henry Dixon, from Marshall (a town named for the former Chief Justice) was famous as the only man in Fauquier County to have voted for Abraham Lincoln in 1860. People said he "carried a pistol in one hand and a ballot in the other." But the divisions that had split the United States were nonetheless duplicated here in the Piedmont—in individual communities and sometimes even within families. In Waterford, Virginia, this struggle had additional poignancy due to the

JAMES GETTY, AN ABRAHAM LINCOLN reenactor, participates annually in Gettysburg's Remembrance Day Parade, held on the Saturday closest to November 19, the anniversary of Lincoln's 1863 Gettysburg Address. On the 19th itself, an additional ceremony is held at the Gettysburg National Cemetery, where a famous speaker holds forth each year.

UNION REENACTORS, ACCOMPANIED by fifes and drums, as well as camp followers and dignitaries, march down Route 15, Gettysburg's main street, as the entire town turns out in full force for the Remembrance Day Parade.

tenets of its founders, the pacifist Quakers. Village elders of this town, the second most prosperous in the region before the war, wrestled with whether they should refuse to bear arms or take a stand in the name of freedom and racial equality. At last a local miller, Sam Means, raised a cavalry militia, the Loudoun Rangers, as the only battalion in Virginia to join the Union. On August 26, 1862, he occupied the Baptist church as his headquarters. While Means was home visiting his family, the church was attacked by a unit in the Virginia Cavalry's 35th Battalion, commanded by local farmer Elijah White. Among the besieged was Charles Smoots; his brother William was one of the Confederate soldiers shooting at him.

After a three-hour firefight, which was occasionally interrupted by cease-fires while local residents ferried surrender demands to the church, the Rangers ran low on ammunition and surrendered to Captain White. As the Union troops were being disarmed, William Smoots made one last attempt to shoot his brother Charles but was stopped by a Confederate officer. It was a brutal war, and, as the Union forces invading Virginia soon discovered, it was not going to be cheap.

Meanwhile, the Dutton sisters, Lizzie and Lida, and friend Sarah Steer undertook a dangerous task to support the Union. The three young women published the *Waterford News*, "to cheer the weary soldier, and render material aid to the sick and wounded." They also sought to spread and reinforce the concept of freedom for all. "We feel a great interest in the affairs of our country and we shall with our humble ability advocate the union of States and freedom of person as well as opinion." They published eight editions in 1865, the last year of the war, and raised a thousand dollars for the Sanitary Commission, to treat wounded soldiers. After the war, Sarah Steer formed a public school for the black children of Waterford.

The pacifism of the larger Quaker community ultimately hurt the Waterford Quakers. After the war, Virginia leaders intentionally ensured that the tracks for a major new railroad line were not laid to the prosperous town because most of the Quakers had refused to fight. As a result, most Waterford residents lost their businesses and died in ruin; slowly, the once thriving town became desolate.

In the early months of the war, as both sides rushed to turn hordes of enthusiastic volunteers into soldiers, the Union commanders were being urged to "crush" the Confederate forces around Manassas. The area was just a few miles east of Bull Run Mountain, the first of the Blue Ridge foothills, and a vital railroad junction for the Southerners, linking lines from the Shenandoah Valley and the Deep South. Accordingly, a Union army marched out in July 1861 to do battle, followed by onlookers from Washington. Among them was William Howard Russell, a war correspondent for the *Times* of London. "In an hour more we had gained the high road to Centreville," he wrote, "on which were many ... wagons full of civilians, and ... the slopes of the hill ... covered with men, carts and horses, and the summit crested with spectators ... gazing on the valley beyond."

Initial reports spoke of a Union victory, and the spectators shouted, "Bully for us! Bravo! Didn't I tell you so?" But nearer the front lines Russell met a stream of fleeing Union soldiers shouting, "Turn back! Turn back! We are whipped." Following the retreating troops, Russell suddenly heard artillery open fire nearby. "In an instant the mass of vehicles and retreating soldiers, teamsters and civilians, as if agonized by an electric shock, quivered through the tortuous line. With dreadful shouts and cursings, the drivers lashed their maddened horses, [or] leaping from the carts, left them to their fate and ran on foot."

THIS PARCEL-GILT, SILVER, ENAMEL, and diamond ceremonial sword from Tiffany & Co. was presented to a Union soldier who fought in the Virginia campaign under the Army of the Potomac.

Both sides were highly disorganized in this First Battle of Bull Run, but the Union side panicked and collapsed first, producing both a smashing success for the Confederates and a general belief that the Southerners were better fighters.

A few months later, in October 1861, a Union attempt to outflank the Confederates on the Piedmont from the north led to a minor disaster at a point on the Potomac called Ball's Bluff when Union forces tried to cross. As many as half the Union forces were killed or drowned, and some of the bodies floated down the river all the way to Washington, D.C. Soon after the incident, a shocked Congress began searching out scapegoats for the North's repeated military failures.

THE LINCOLN ADDRESS MEMORIAL stands some 300 yards from where his actual speech—commonly known as the Gettysburg Address—was given. Abraham Lincoln's craggy features seem to evoke the wise words he spoke in his historic address to the thousands of people who attended the dedication of the Gettysburg National Cemetery on November 19, 1863: "The world will little note nor long remember what we say here, but it can never forget what they did here...." The speech's simplicity, truthfulness, straightforwardness, and timeliness forged the foundation for the building of a single nation, once the war ended a year and a half later, and in spite of the brutal assassination of a heroic and long-suffering President.

REMEMBRANCE DAY AT GETTYSBURG
War widows' black veils are caught in the breeze as reenactors
walk along the Remembrance Day parade route on Baltimore Street.
Twin Sycamores, a house built in the 1820s, is in the background.

The following summer, the Union Army, now commanded by Gen. George B. McClellan, attempted a roundabout approach with 100,000 men to reach Richmond via the Tidewater. However, within six miles of the Confederate capital his chronic indecision compelled him to break off the fight and return home again. With Lee in command, the Confederates then took the offensive in the Piedmont, and in August they outmaneuvered the Union Army, again at Manassas. The decisive moment in the battle came when the Confederate force under Gen. James Longstreet emerged unexpectedly from behind Bull Run Mountain through a narrow pass called Thoroughfare Gap and crashed into the Union left flank.

THIS WAS ONE OF THE MOST CELEBRATED CONFEDERATE victories of the war, but such triumphs tended to be ruinous for anyone who lived on the spot. The early stages of the Second Battle of Bull Run (or the Second Battle of Manassas, as the Confederacy called it) were centered on the home of a poor tenant farmer, John Brawner, because a Confederate officer decided his house would be suitable as a defensive strongpoint. Brawner later recalled how he, his wife, and their three daughters fled as the "house was shelled and balls [were] passing through the house." His daughter Mary left a succinct account of what it was like living between two armies: "Part of the time we were in the Confederate lines. When the southern army fell back we were within the Union lines. The Union army was passing backwards and forwards all the time after the southern army left. We were not able to cultivate the farm after the first year. We raised a small crop in 1862 … [and that] was lost at the time of the battle."

The fight around the Brawner farm was only a small part of the Second Battle of Bull Run. It lasted just 90 minutes, during which men from Virginia, Indiana, Wisconsin, and New York blazed away at each other with muzzle-loading muskets and rifles from lines only 70 to 80 yards apart, leaving a total of 2,375 men killed, wounded, or missing. A careful modern-day search of a field that was occupied for part of the battle by an Indiana regiment revealed the degree to which these Civil War soldiers fought without regard for their own safety. Thanks to the distribution of unfired musket balls dropped by men fumbling to reload, as well as the nearby remains of other shells and bullets that had been fired at them, it became clear that these long-dead Indiana soldiers, rather than firing from behind a ridge in the field for protection, had instead been standing a few yards farther forward, on top of the ridge and therefore fully exposed.

CONSIDERING WHAT THEY ROUTINELY ENDURED, IT IS A wonder that troops of either side stood their ground at all. Although military technology had made many advances in the years before the war, including repeating rifles and breech-loading cannon, generals on both sides fought in the style of the Napoleonic wars half a century earlier, with massed ranks marching across open ground amid a rain of fire and cacophany. Survivors remembered the clang of the Union Army's 12-pound "Napoleon" cannon and the "solid deep-toned bumble bee-like 'z-z-z-z-z-z-zip'" of the minié-ball rifle bullets that ended with an echoing slap as they hit a target.

Wounded men had to lie where they fell until nightfall or longer. One description of the aftermath of an 1864 battle south of the Rappahannock said the "writhing of the wounded and dying who

THE RED BARN IN THIS FIELD north of Gettysburg marks an area that would have been in the thick of fighting on the first day of the Battle of Gettysburg, when the Confederate troops moved down from the north. The town of Gettysburg can be seen in the distance.

PICKETT'S CHARGE
Union and Confederate troops reenact the July 3, 1863, action known as Pickett's Charge. It marked the last gasp of Confederate efforts, turned the tide in favor of the Union, and affected the outcome of the war.

JOHN LATSCHAR

PEOPLE ARE THIRSTY TO UNDERSTAND OUR NATION'S PAST, WHICH IS WHY WE HAVE SUCH A TREMENDOUS GROWTH IN "HERITAGE TOURISM." PEOPLE ... WANT TO LEARN SOMETHING WHILE STILL HAVING A GOOD TIME.

John Latschar has been the superintendent of Gettysburg National Military Park since 1994. He oversees a permanent and seasonal staff that includes rangers, interpreters, and cultural resource specialists.

"We think Gettysburg is the most popular of the Civil War battlefield sites for three principal reasons. First of all, there is a vast popular perception that Gettysburg was the turning point of the Civil War. Second, Abraham Lincoln chose this site to deliver the Gettysburg Address ... which defined the Civil War for his generation and defines the meaning of freedom for us today. Third ... Gettysburg is the battlefield that symbolizes the reconciliation of the white North and South. When time had passed following the war, this was by far the most popular place for ... reunions among veterans from both sides. This climaxed at the 50th anniversary in 1913, when veterans from North and South shook hands across the stone wall on Cemetery Ridge, the site of Pickett's Charge. At that meeting, which was a huge national

John Latschar, superintendent,
Gettysburg National Military Park

celebration ... the veterans agreed that there should be a national peace memorial to symbolize the fact that this nation would never go to war with itself again.

"Our principal mission is to preserve the battlefield—unimpaired—for future generations to observe and enjoy, and understand what went on here. Our long-range plan is to make it possible for visitors to understand both the decisions made by the generals, and also understand what the soldiers endured. To that end, we are working to restore the landscape of the battlefield as much as possible to the condition it was in back in 1863. For example, removing woods that were not there at that time, and replanting those that were. We also work ...to persuade local communities and local governments of the importance of preserving the historic landscape surrounding the battlefield itself. Today, more and more people are thirsty to understand our nation's past, which is why we have such a tremendous growth in 'heritage tourism.' People want something more than just recreation; they want to learn something while still having a good time."

lay beneath the dead bodies moved the whole mass." In the beginning, at least, they had little hope of professional medical care. Clara Barton was working at the U.S. Patent Office in Washington in 1861 when she heard there was no medical system for the wounded. The clever and intrepid Barton, who had previously started the first free public school in New Jersey, was drawing the regular salary for her position at the U.S. Patent Office—not a decreased woman's rate, as was customary. Applying this same determination to the task of creating medical support for the soldiers, she began collecting money for bandages and other necessities and lobbied the Army to grant her permission to bring them to the battlefields. After a year, with the help of Senator Henry Wilson of Massachusetts, she persuaded the Army bureaucracy to let her travel with the ambulances. Barton's legacy of medical support in time of crisis formed the foundation for the eventual establishment of the American Red Cross. Nevertheless, even if they received first aid on the battlefield, men were twice as likely to die of disease in their unsanitary camps as of their injuries in battle. Of the 630,000 Civil War deaths, 414,000 were from typhoid, dysentery, tuberculosis, or other illnesses.

A month after his victory at Manassas, Lee crossed the Potomac into Maryland, a Union state, partly because he wanted to give the farmers of Virginia a chance to reap the fall harvest without interference from marauding armies. In the meantime he could feed his hungry troops from the lush farms of Maryland. More important, he was mindful of the outside audience watching the war in this theater. The Confederates pinned their hopes for independence on getting official recognition from the European powers, and by the summer of 1862 it looked as if the British were on the brink of intervening in what the London *Times* was calling "a scandal to humanity." A successful invasion of the North, or at least another impressive victory, might clinch the matter.

Part of Lee's plan was to recapture Harpers Ferry, the key to control of the northern Shenandoah Valley. Occupied and then abandoned by Confederate and Union troops early in the war, the town was left unoccupied by either side but blockaded by the South in the fall and winter of 1861. Most of the inhabitants had fled, and for those who were left, said resident Annie Marmion, the blockade, "threatened starvation [and] desolation inconceivable." When Union forces returned early in 1862 they found the place "a picture of desolation." One telling clue to the ruin wrought by the war hides

A CONFEDERATE CANNON

(opposite, top) faces the open ground where Pickett's Charge took place. Two cannon shots were fired that morning to signal the start of a bombardment, which filled the valley with smoke. When ammunition began to run low, Gen. E. P. Alexander ordered the charge, in which most of the men were shot down after emerging near enemy lines where the smoke had cleared. A Virginia state monument designed by Louis Comfort Tiffany commemorates the debacle with the blowing of a bugle (opposite, bottom).

A MONUMENT AT BALL'S BLUFF

National Cemetery recognizes the heroism of Col. Edward Baker, a longtime friend of Lincoln's and the only standing U.S. senator to be killed in the line of fire. Numerous Union soldiers were pushed back into the Potomac River during the battle, and their bodies floated down to Washington, where Lincoln came to the harsh realization that the war would most likely continue for a long time.

BATTLE OF CEDAR MOUNTAIN
At this battlefield, now a bucolic park, on Route 15 near Culpeper, Virginia, Stonewall Jackson's Confederates were victorious over Gen. John Pope's Union Army in August 1862.

DAGUERREOTYPES LIKE THESE OF
a Union trooper (top) and of a Confederate cavalryman (bottom), were commonly taken before young men left for war, to be given in parting to their mothers, wives, or sweethearts. In return, loved ones often gave their own images, to be gazed upon nostalgically while the men served on battlefields far from home.

CHARCOAL SKETCHES ARE
discernible on the walls of the Graffiti House (opposite), a triage hospital near the railroad at Brandy Station, Virginia, site of the war's largest cavalry battle. While waiting for transfer to a larger facility, soldiers often sketched. Here a woman lifts her skirts, perhaps picking her way over rough terrain after watching a battle.

in the soil there today. Pollen samples studied by archaeologists conclusively demonstrate that the town's lush grass lawns disappeared, replaced everywhere by weeds.

Dispatched by Lee, Stonewall Jackson recaptured Harpers Ferry without too much difficulty, but then he had to hurry to rejoin the rest of the army thanks to the unexpected appearance of the Army of the Potomac under McClellan. On September 17, 1862, the two sides met at Antietam Creek, near the Maryland town of Sharpsburg. That same day, reports of the second Union defeat at Manassas finally reached London. "The time is come," wrote the British foreign secretary in reaction to the news, "for offering mediation to the United States Gov't, with a view to the recognition of the independence of the Confederates." Lincoln, meanwhile, had prepared an Emancipation Proclamation that effectively pledged the Union to abolish slavery, but felt he could not announce it without a Union victory. One way or another, the impending clash would be a turning point in the struggle.

"The night was close, air heavy ... some rainfall," recalled a Pennsylvania private of the eve of battle. "The air was perfumed with a mixture of crushed green corn stalks, ragweed, and clover. We made our beds between rows of corn and would not remove our accouterments." Following the day-long fight, the fields were "plowed with shot, watered with blood, and sown thick with dead," wrote a reporter, while over the entire landscape, "the sultry air was laden with the smoke of gunpowder and of the smoldering ruins of burnt houses and barns and straw piles. The fields were ploughed by cannon balls and strewed thick with all manner of debris. Fences were demolished, and rails in splinters; the green corn blades were in shreds and trampled into the dust. The trees of the woods looked as if they had been threshed with a giant's flail." Of the 132,000 men there that day, nearly one in five lay dead or wounded. The battle had the largest number of casualties of any battle in America's history—23,000 killed, wounded, or missing in a single day.

THIS CONFEDERATE CAVALRYMAN'S
firearm is a two-piece pistol carbine, adapted
for either close-up or long-distance shooting.
It displays the date 1862 and the word Fay-
etteville, indicating that it was manufactured
in North Carolina, with machinery captured
at the Harpers Ferry arsenal in 1861, before
the Confederates burned the arsenal.

Some units lost more than half their strength. One Maine regiment, ordered to drive away enemy who were "annoying" Union artillery batteries, lost 100 of their 181 officers and men. Retreating into an orchard under enemy fire, they found "the twigs and branches of the apple trees were being cut off by musket balls, and were dropping in a shower." The order to attack, said the regimental commander bitterly, came "from no plan or design from headquarters, but from an inspiration of John Barleycorn [whiskey] in our Brigade Commander alone." Later, an awestruck British visitor found that "in about seven or eight acres of wood there is not a tree which is not full of bullets and bits of shell. It is impossible to understand how anyone could live in such a fire."

Among those in the line of fire was Clara Barton, who had arrived from Washington with a wagonload of bandages and other supplies and immediately began helping the wounded with food and drink. "A man lying upon the ground asked for drink," she wrote later. "I stooped to give it, and having raised him with my right hand, was holding the cup to his lips with my left, when I felt a sudden twitch of the loose sleeve of my dress—the poor fellow sprang from my hands and fell back quivering in the agonies of death—a ball had passed

between my body and the right arm which supported him—cutting through the sleeve, and passing through his chest from shoulder to shoulder."

At several moments during the day the out-numbered Confederates were on the point of giving way, but typically, McClellan was too fearful to commit his reserves, and Lee survived. He did, however, give up his Maryland campaign and retreat south again, giving the Union a strategic success. News of the battle's outcome flashed around the country by telegraph and crossed the Atlantic within two weeks (there was no transatlantic wire), causing the pro-southern *Times* newspaper to pronounce Lee's inva-sion "a failure." Talk of British intervention faded away, and when Lincoln, buoyed by the victory, made good on his proclamation, it disappeared forever. "Recognition of the South, by England whilst it bases itself on Negro slavery," wrote a pro-Union British politician, "is an impossibility."

Meanwhile, at Antietam the land not only looked ruined, it smelled. For days people living miles away kept their doors and windows closed against the stench, which came in part from the decomposing carcasses of thousands of horses. Horses were everywhere on the battlefields. Each artillery gun, for example, required a team of 12 to pull the cannon and its accompanying caisson. Naturally, enemy artillery horses were prime targets for sharpshooters and gunners.

Above all, there were the bodies of those who had made the ultimate sacrifice in the struggle. A Pennsylvania soldier assigned to burial duty at Antietam wrote: "The weather was phenomenally hot, and the stench from the hundreds of black, bloated, decomposed magotty bodies, exposed to a torrid heat for three days after the battle, was a sight truly horrid....Overhead floated large numbers of those harpies of the air, buzzards, awaiting an opportunity to descend to earth to partake of the cadaverous feast." Most of the dead were hurriedly buried where they fell. Many were later properly interred in marked graves, but farmers plowing their fields continued to turn up human bones for years to come.

A TYPICAL MEDICAL KIT OF THE TIME (above) focuses on amputation equipment consisting of various knives and saws. A likeness of the physician who owned the case rests inside. Contrary to legendary horror stories of legions of men suffering amputation while fully conscious, anesthetics were used whenever they were available. During the war, wounded soldiers stayed at the Exchange Hotel in Gordonsville, Virginia (opposite), which until then had served passengers on the Virginia Central Railroad and the Alexandria Railroad. As a care facility, it aided 70,000 troops from both sides. Today the fully restored hotel serves as a Civil War–era museum.

A CIVIL WAR MEDICAL MUSEUM IN downtown Frederick, Maryland, shows how medicine was practiced on Civil War battlefields. The focus on amputations is particularly revealing. In most cases little could be done to save injured limbs, and they had to be removed. Note the copper funnel over the nose of the amputee— ether was available as an anesthetic, contrary to the commonly held myth that there was none.

In the midst of this misery, one of the significant documents of American history transformed thousands of lives, and in fact, had an impact on all Americans. Following the battle, on January 1, 1863, President Lincoln issued the Emancipation Proclamation, an act to establish "that all persons held as slaves" within the Confederate states "are, and henceforward shall be free."

THE AFTERMATH OF WAR WAS FRAUGHT WITH ITS OWN kind of conflict. three months later, in December 1862, the Union's Army of the Potomac headed south, crossing the Rappahannock in boats below the fords. They occupied Fredericksburg, the sleepy old tobacco port, and comprehensively sacked it. George Washington Lane, a fisherman in civilian life from Massachusetts, wrote unapologetically to his wife that "all the folks left the sity and the [soldiers] took perseson of the houses every man had a house of his [own]." The soldiers would say, "This is nothing but a sesech [secessionist, or Rebel] house" and use all the furniture, including beds and chairs, as fuel for their cooking fires. The destruction left a legacy of bitterness—a century later, Northerners were still treated with chilly hostility in the city—and at the time the southern press called it "the most infamous crime ever perpetrated upon this continent." This sort of thing had been routine in the Piedmont country districts for 18 months, but the plunder of a genteel little town seemed more heinous.

Outraged Confederates took their revenge when the Federals attacked south of the town. The advancing blue-uniformed ranks were mown down by well-situated defenders, leading to another Union defeat. When the Union commander, Gen. Ambrose Burnside (McClellan had been fired for excessive caution after Antietam), concluded that frontal assaults against a dug-in enemy were not a good idea and tried to maneuver around Lee's western flank, Lee outmaneuvered him at Chancellorsville—one of the worst Union defeats so far.

Meanwhile, inland, the Piedmont was becoming a dangerous no-man's-land. Even without major armies moving back and forth, farmers were very much at the mercy of deserters and other stragglers living off the land. Willis Madden, the free African American who had built up his prosperous tavern outside Culpeper through sweat and guile, was still managing to keep his business going, but the war was getting closer all the time; in the winter of 1862-63, both armies set up their winter camps on opposite sides of the Rappahannock River, each warily watching the other. These camps, with as many as 120,000 troops, were the largest of the Civil War, and their impact on Culpeper was devastating. In February 1863, during a raging blizzard, a small group of Confederate officers knocked on Madden's door, looking for shelter. Madden had no hesitation in slamming the door in their faces, saying he wanted "nothing to do with no stragglers." One of the party was Maj. John Pelham, a rising star in the Confederate artillery, known as "the gallant Pelham" for his actions at Fredericksburg. Only when they knocked again, claiming that one of them (in reality a German mercenary) was Robert E. Lee himself and another the "French ambassador," did Madden let them in and feed them. The party rode away the next day, congratulating themselves on having fooled a "stupid old nigger," as Madden's family recorded, perhaps without reflecting on how smart a black man would have to be to keep a business going in a slave state, in a war zone.

A month later Pelham was killed in a cavalry charge in a battle at Kelly's Ford a few miles from Madden's tavern. Not long afterward, there was a firefight between Union and Confederate troops at Germanna Ford, still closer to Madden, which spilled over onto his land. In June came the cavalry battle at nearby Brandy Station. The 9,000-man Confederate cavalry commanded by Gen. J.E.B. Stuart had been camped on the rolling grass meadows there. They had even staged a flamboyant parade for General Lee himself and all his staff before being surprised by an attack of 10,000 Union cavalry, who had forded the river thinking they were merely facing a Rebel raiding party of unknown strength. The result was the largest-scale cavalry fight ever in North America, but although the northern force fought well, they pulled back across the river without discovering Lee's main army camped nearby around Culpeper.

In fact, Lee was about to move north across the Potomac into Union territory again, calculating that his near defeat at Antietam had been a lucky fluke for McClellan and that this time he could win a decisive victory that would force Lincoln to negotiate. He was also again eager to relieve the Virginia farmers at the expense of those in Maryland and Pennsylvania. Slipping through the Blue

Ridge into the Shenandoah Valley, he turned toward Maryland. Stuart's cavalry stayed east of the Blue Ridge, fighting a series of battles—Aldie, Middleburg, Upperville—as he screened the northward march of his commander on the other side of the mountains. Meanwhile, the Union Army, to Lee's surprise, was in hot pursuit of him. Eventually, the two sides met at Gettysburg, east of South Mountain. Over three days, 150,000 men fought in a brutal struggle that ultimately determined the course of the war. On the first day, the Confederates appeared to have won one of their customary victories, attacking from the north (they had reached deep into Pennsylvania) and driving the Union forces back through the prosperous town of Gettysburg, into the long ridgeline to the south. There, on the second and third day, the Confederate forces assaulted the defending Unionists, who were ably commanded by Gen. George Meade. The names of places in the line would become part of American history—Culp's Hill, Cemetery Ridge, Little Round Top. At various times the Confederates seemed near to success. During the second night of the battle, for example, the troops fighting their way up though the woods on Culp's Hill on the far right of the Union line came within a few yards of cutting the

CONFEDERATES CHARGE UNION LINES (opposite) during a reenactment of the battle at Antietam. Union troops (below) fire back simultaneously, enveloping themselves in a cloud of smoke.

A YOUNG REENACTOR
This ten-year-old boy traveled all the way from Texas to practice his reenacting skills as a Union soldier at the Gettysburg battlefield. He stands with sword in hand at Big Round Top as the sun sets over the Valley of Death in the background.

THE 1797-BUILT CASHTOWN INN, just west of Gettysburg, off Route 30, owes its name to its first owner's policy of cash only for goods as well as the tolls he collected from travelers. Cashtown sits at the northern end of the 175-mile stretch of Hallowed Ground where so much of the nation's history was made. The town where Cashtown Inn lies took its name from the inn, which provided "for the entertainment of strangers and travelers."

During the Civil War, the inn and town found themselves overrun by hundreds of strangers when J.E.B. Stuart's Confederate cavalry briefly occupied the town in October 1862, and again the next summer when Robert E. Lee ordered his Army of Northern Virginia to regroup at Cashtown to defend Confederate supply lines against approaching Union troops. The inn also served as headquarters at this time for Confederate Gen. A. P. Hill. For a number of days in June and July of 1863, Cashtown's community became a Confederate camp and the inn a recuperation site for the 37-year-old Hill, who suffered from a chronic illness. While there, the Confederate commissaries baked bread in the large ovens in the cellar of the inn, and Hill likely bathed in the clear spring water that also ran through the cellar. The wounded were treated throughout the town in homes and even stables.

At this reenactment, Robert Boswell, posing as Confederate President Jefferson Davis, stands between two Union soldiers. (Davis never actually visited Gettysburg.) A woman with veil and hooped skirt—perhaps a bride—entertains others on the veranda. Traditionally, on the weekend nearest the Gettysburg campaign's anniversary the management hosts a festival and concert, sponsored by the Second Maryland Confederate reenactors, during which a fife-and-drum jam session takes place to Civil War–era tunes. The grand old inn, recently given a major structural overhaul, is still in operation as a bed-and-breakfast and restaurant. Its Victorian dining room and original tavern room offer American cuisine.

Union supply lifeline but did not know it. Little Round Top, at the other end of the line, was occupied by Union troops mere minutes before the Confederates moved in to take possession.

Almost every survivor's account conveys something of the fearsome intensity of the battle. Robert Stiles, for example, a Yale graduate from Kentucky who had joined the Confederate artillery, was ordered across the battlefield on the third day to deliver an urgent message. "One of the horrors of the thing during a large part of the ride," he wrote in his memoir, "was that I could see almost every shell that passed, as they were coming straight toward me.... As I approached the points at which the fire was directed ... the number of projectiles and explosions increased—until at last there was absolutely no separation between the reports, but the air was rent by one continuous shriek and roar of explosion and torn with countless myriads of hurtling fragments."

Repulsed on the left and the right of the Union front, Lee on the third day ordered an infantry charge against the enemy center, across open ground and up a slope against massed ranks of the enemy, who were shooting from behind a stone wall—an assault that became famous as Pickett's Charge. As so often happened in the Civil War battles, smoke from the black powder used by both sides clung so thickly on the ground that in some places the advancing troops could not even see the enemy until they were within 200 yards of the Union line. Their ranks shredded by torrents of rifle fire and artillery, very few of the attackers reached the line itself, and those who did were quickly killed or thrown back.

On July 9, just days after Pickett's Charge, a relatively small but critical battle raged at Monocacy Junction in Frederick County, Maryland. Confederate Lt. Gen. Jubal Early was headed toward Washington, at Lee's command, with 15,000 troops. On his way, he planned to take control of Monocacy Junction, a major station of the Baltimore and Ohio Railroad, and take the town of Frederick. Though the day-long Battle of Monocacy resulted in a Confederate victory, it delayed the southern forces long enough for the Union to mobilize defense of the District. It was thus forever known as the "Battle That Saved Washington."

THIS PARCEL-GILT AND STEEL SWORD was custom-made in Richmond by Mitchell and Tyler Manufacturers for the occasion of Robert E. Lee's grand review of the Confederate Army in June 1863. It was presented to Maj. Gen. J.E.B. Stuart by his chief of staff, Harris von Borcke.

TWO CONFEDERATE BELT BUCKLES bear the initials "CS" for Confederate States, and the middle one sports the seal of the Commonwealth of Virginia.

PICKETT'S CHARGE HAD BEEN LEE'S LAST VALIANT EFFORT. Following the failure of the charge he pulled his army off the field and began retracing his steps back to the south and safety, easily fending off Meade's desultory efforts to pursue him. The battlefield was littered with thousands of bodies, and the people of Gettysburg urgently needed them buried—thousands of soldiers and 5,000 horses. Those clinging to life were transported to "hospitals" in churches, schools, and other buildings until Camp Letterman General Hospital could be set up near Gettysburg. This hospital, a series of large tents, served as a triage and way station for transport to hospitals in Philadelphia, Baltimore, and Washington. Some 20,000 wounded soldiers on both sides were treated on their way through Camp Letterman. One was 72-year-old Gettysburg resident John Burns, a veteran of the War of 1812. His commitment to his country is immortalized in a statue that stands at the park.

For Gettysburg's dead, initial plans to create a locally owned war cemetery gave way to a more ambitious scheme worthy of the great Union victory, for a "National Cemetery" to hold the dead. (Union dead, that is. Confederate dead were left where they lay, with a few shovelfuls of earth thrown over them.) By fall, with the armies far away, all was ready for the inauguration of the burial ground, on the summit of a hill next to an existing cemetery that had been on the front lines during the battle. Edward Everett, the most famous orator of the day, was to give the keynote address, while President Lincoln was to deliver some "dedicatory remarks."

On the day, November 19, 1863, Everett spoke for two hours to the 15,000 people who had streamed into town for the ceremony, Lincoln for two minutes. But in just 272 words he redefined the purpose of America as a nation, as well as the cause for which the Union soldiers had died, in terms of the Founding Fathers' "perfect idea" that all men are created equal, a central principle overriding the careful balancing of rights and interests of a Constitution that sanctioned slavery: "Four score and seven years ago our fathers brought forth on this continent a new nation, conceived in Liberty, and dedicated to the proposition that all men are created equal...." In other words, the fight was not simply about preserving a collective union of states,

THIS IMAGE OF ROBERT E. LEE WAS recently discovered in a trunk owned by his wife, and was housed for years in the basement of the Burke and Herbert Bank in Alexandria, Virginia. Uncovered with the photograph were the three stars of his insignia (seen here on his uniform). The gold stars were cut off Lee's uniform at the surrender to General Grant in Appomattox. Lee negotiated with Grant that his soldiers be permitted to wear their uniforms home as long as they cut off all insignia, since the soldiers had no other clothes. The stars were found wrapped in a letter addressed to Miss Belle Harrison from the general, dated May 5, 1865. In it he says he wanted to give her the stars to remind her of him. Isabella Ritchie Harrison of Prince George County, Virginia, was a Lee family friend, who lived until 1895.

MOSBY HERITAGE AREA
The sun casts a hopeful glow over rolling hills and lush farmland outside Upperville, Virginia. This land, once traversed on horseback by John Mosby and his raiders, was the center of Mosby's activities.

GAYLE DELASHMUTT

JOHN MOSBY WOULD STILL RECOGNIZE A LOT OF THE AREA IF HE WERE TO RIDE OVER IT TODAY. FROM ROUTE 15 WEST UP TO THE BLUE RIDGE MOUNTAINS AND OVER TO THE SHENANDOAH, YOU CAN STILL GO DOWN VILLAGE STREETS THAT LOOK MUCH THE SAME AS DURING THE TIME OF THE CIVIL WAR.

Gayle DeLashmutt is president of the Mosby Heritage Area Association, an organization dedicated to educating about, and advocating for, preservation of the historic region comprising Loudoun, the western tip of Prince William, Fauquier, Clark, and Warren Counties within Virginia. She and her family live at Oak Hill, the Loudon County, Virginia, home designed by Thomas Jefferson and built by James Monroe. Although the home is not open to the public, they occasionally host events for educators.

"Our mission is preservation through education. We're trying to bring awareness to our 1,800-square-mile area, the area that John Singleton Mosby rode and raided. We're trying to bring awareness of the natural and historic resources in the area not only to the people that live here and love it and are protecting it, but also to visitors. We're just one cog in the wheel of the many associations out here that work to preserve the area. In this one area there are sixteen historic districts, four national historic landmarks, forty-four state national historic sites, and six Civil War battlefields. One of those historic landmarks is the entire village of Waterford, and if you were reincarnated from the era of the 1860s and walked down the main street you would pretty much know where you were. Oak Hill is another historic landmark [although] it's a working farm, currently about 1,200 acres, raising cattle and corn.

"John Mosby would still recognize a lot of the area if he were to ride over it today. From Route 15 West up to the Blue Ridge Mountains and over to the Shenandoah, you can still go down village streets that look much the same as during the time of the Civil War.

"One quirky piece of Mosby history that people find interesting because of the several farms associated with it, is the 'greenback raid.' He held up a payroll for the Union Army, and each of his rangers got $6,000. I most enjoy our work to encourage local people, and especially children, to become active stewards of this historic landscape. We achieve this by visiting schools, publishing maps and guides, speaking to civic groups, offering guided tours, and presenting programs to the public."

Gayle DeLashmutt, president,
Mosby Heritage Area Association

THIS JACKET FROM A PRIVATE COLLECTION is the only one still existing that is known to have been worn by Gen. Ulysses S. Grant during the war. Most of the rest of his wardrobe did not survive. During the Civil War, Grant's movements were carefully monitored, even by northern sympathizers living in the South.

Three Quaker women from Waterford, Virginia—Sarah Steer, plus sisters Lizzie and Lida Dutton—published a newspaper called the Waterford News (pages 111-112), which they succeeded in printing in Maryland and distributing widely, including within Confederate lines. In spite of the risk they took of being apprehended, they produced eight editions of the four-page newspaper, spanning almost a year, and sold it for ten cents a copy until the war ended. Some copies were delivered to Abraham Lincoln, and Horace Greeley's New York Tribune gave it high praise.

The following excerpt from a poem about Grant was published on July 2, 1864, in Vol. 1, No. 3: "Grant him, we pray thee, / Both wisdom and might, / To crush this rebellion / And put Treason to flight; / Grant each day may add laurels / To his bright wreath of fame, / And GRANT, in the future, / Be a world-renowned name."

but about something more fundamental: the survival of a nation, unique in the world, that practiced "government of the people, by the people, for the people." One modern scholar has written of the address that the 15,000 people who heard it "walked off from those curving graves on the hillside, under a changed sky, into a different America."

Of the dead so honored by Lincoln, 102 were buried by Elizabeth Thorn, the pregnant wife of the cemetery caretaker. Her house had been on the Union front line and after the battle was surrounded by dead horses. "It was only excitement that helped me to do all the work," she said later, "with all that stench." Despite promises, she was never paid.

African Americans, who were denied burial rights at National Cemetery, had their own place of rest. About 30 black soldiers of the U.S. Colored Troops were interred at nearby Lincoln Cemetery, including Lloyd Watts and Isaac Buckmaster, who served the Union Army in support of their country and their own freedom. About 198,000 African Americans fought for the North in all.

Meanwhile, following Gettysburg, the Union Army had moved into Culpeper County in the central Piedmont, a development that proved disastrous for Willis Madden, the tavernkeeper. Successive foraging parties gradually stripped him clean. His horses and cart were taken, along with his livestock. Finally, they seized the fences on his property and cut down his three-acre wood to build their own shelters. Ironically, Madden had been ruined by the same army pledged to free his people from subjection and slavery.

While northern troops occupied the Piedmont countryside, they were open to the attacks of Confederate partisans. The most famous was John Singleton Mosby, a Warrenton lawyer and pre-war opponent of secession who joined the Confederate cavalry. His "Partisan Rangers" were irregular troops who lived off the countryside, equipped with weapons and horses they supplied themselves or captured from the enemy. Their only supplies from Richmond, Mosby claimed, were their Confederate uniform jackets. His favored weapon was the six-shooter revolver. He disdained the sabers of the regular cavalry as good only for grilling meat over the fire.

From the spring of 1863, he conducted a highly successful campaign of raiding enemy supply lines, derailing and robbing trains, and carrying off large numbers of prisoners and booty. As he wrote

A MEDALLION FOR THE BATTLE OF Big Bethel at Hampton Roads, Virginia, on June 10, 1861, was presented to Frank M. Burbeck by his father in honor of his son's participation in one of the first battles of the war.

THESE UNION BRASS BUTTONS were captured in the vicinity of Warrenton, Virginia, and brought home after the war by A. D. Payne, Confederate captain of the Black Horse Troop, Company H, Fourth Virginia Cavalry.

in his memoirs: "My purpose was to weaken the armies invading Virginia, by harassing their rear.... To destroy supply trains, to break up the means of conveying intelligence.... It is just as legitimate to fight an enemy in the rear as in the front. The only difference is in the danger."

In a war marked by large-scale battles and remorseless slaughter, the exploits of the "Gray Ghost" had a romantic flavor. In March 1863, for example, he conceived the bold idea of capturing a Union general, Edwin Stoughton, from the Union base at Centreville. "I then had no reputation to lose even if I failed," he wrote, "and I remembered the motto, 'Adventures to the adventurous.'" He succeeded brilliantly, getting past all the guards to find the general fast asleep in bed, took him prisoner, and got clean away without losing a man or a horse. On the realization that he had done it, Mosby wrote in his memoirs, he "had drawn a prize in the lottery of life."

Mosby evaded determined efforts to catch him and roamed the "Mosby Confederacy," from Leesburg down to Culpeper, from Harpers Ferry to Alexandria, until the end of the war. Mosby retired as an attorney in the Justice Department and lived on until 1916, in old age retelling his saga to a young George Patton, the future World War II commander.

While Mosby had been inconveniencing the Union rear, the Army of the Potomac had pushed remorselessly south under Grant's unwavering determination to destroy Lee's army and with it the rebellion. Some of the bloodier battles of the war were fought south of the Rappahannock in the Wilderness, the great forest of secondary growth that had replaced the trees cut down by Governor Spotswood for his iron furnaces a century before. By early 1865, Lee was blockaded around Richmond by Grant's army, while Sherman's army rampaged across Georgia.

The drama finally ended at Appomattox Court House on April 9, 1865. The surrender there was rich in symbolism; the respect with which Grant treated Lee harkened back to George Washington's own treatment of Hessian prisoners of war during the American Revolution. The United States had been torn asunder, but its founders' principles had endured.

THIS 1869 OIL PAINTING BY
Henry Mosler, entitled "The Lost Cause," portrays the all-too-realistic scene of a Confederate soldier returning to his home abandoned and in ruins after the war. Starting over with very little, if anything, Southerners suffered for many years through Reconstruction and into the 20th century.

GETTYSBURG REMEMBRANCE DAY
At dusk each year at the National Cemetery in Gettysburg on Remembrance Day, luminarias are lighted at each grave. The cemetery is laid out in segments of a semicircle around the National Soldier's Monument. Of the total 22 segments, 18 are for the states of the Union that had soldiers represented, 1 is for U.S. regular troops who fought there, and 3 are for the unknown soldier.

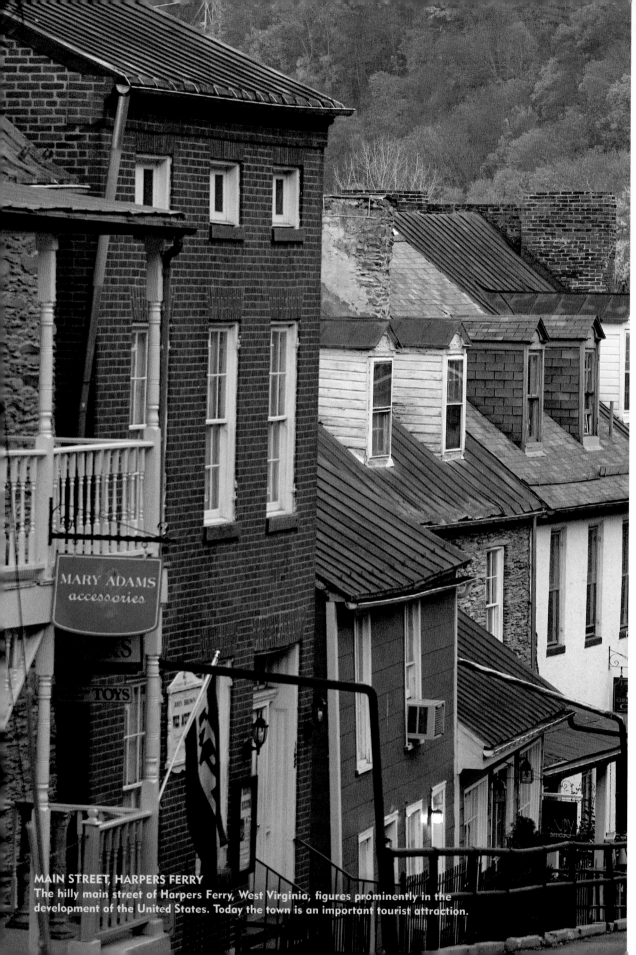

MAIN STREET, HARPERS FERRY
The hilly main street of Harpers Ferry, West Virginia, figures prominently in the
development of the United States. Today the town is an important tourist attraction.

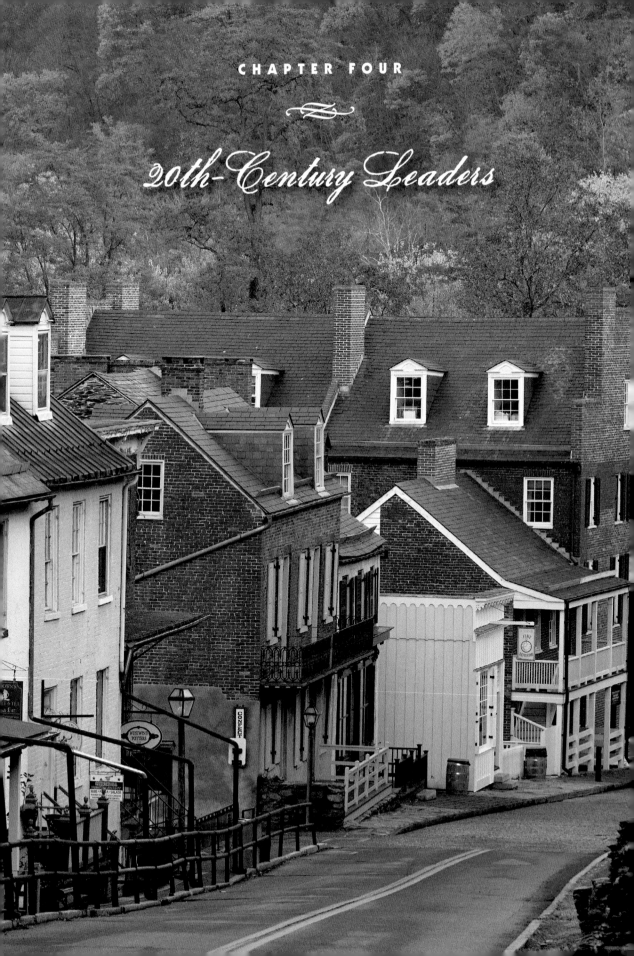

CHAPTER FOUR

20th-Century Leaders

20th-Century Leaders

"AFTER THE READING WE WERE TOLD THAT WE WERE ALL FREE, AND COULD GO WHEN AND WHERE
WE PLEASED. MY MOTHER ... KISSED HER CHILDREN, WHILE TEARS OF JOY RAN DOWN HER CHEEKS."
—BOOKER T. WASHINGTON, EDUCATOR AND ACTIVIST

I asked Grandma how they got along right after the Civil War," wrote Robert Herbert in his memoir about growing up on a Fauquier farm in the 1880s, "when all the slaves had been set free and nearly everything they owned had been taken except one old lame horse called Hopper and all of the farm equipment was destroyed when the Yankees burned the barn. She said: 'The main thing I remember is how glad we were in the

thought that no more of our young men would be killed. This thought made up for a lot of hardships and inconveniences.'"

For those attempting to make a living on the devastated land, this was often the only consoling fact of life. In Warrenton, Virginia, during the winter of 1865, when most people earned one dollar a day, a cord of wood (the only heating and building material) cost five dollars. With the economy in ruins, many people simply picked up stakes and moved west, such as Jacob Mumma, whose land had been fought over at Antietam. Unable to bring his old farm back to prosperity, he moved on to Illinois. Among those who remained behind, especially in what had been Confederate territory, memories of the tumultuous years remained fresh. Recalling his boyhood, Herbert wrote, "I can remember no mention of anything other than current affairs except talk of the Civil War and subjects related thereto."

THERE WAS ONE GROUP, HOWEVER, WHOSE lives had definitely been improved by the war—the slaves. In his autobiography, educator and activist Booker T. Washington recalled the day when, as a small child, he and his fellow slaves on the plantation in Franklin County were set free: "The most distinct thing that I now recall ... was that some man who seemed to be a stranger (a United States officer, I presume) made a little speech and then read a rather long paper.... After the reading we were told that we were all free, and could go when and where we pleased. My mother, who was standing by my side, leaned over and kissed her children, while tears of joy ran down her cheeks."

Although the immediate impulse of most freed slaves, as Washington noted, was to leave the plantation, if only temporarily, "in order that they might really feel sure that they were free," many returned to work the land where they had grown up. As Karen Hughes White, director of the Afro-American Historical Association of Fauquier, said, they had "the skills to survive, they were the ones already working the land, and they were in many cases skilled craftsmen and women." Given their all-too-recent status as legal property of the

HERBERT HOOVER'S FISHING CAMP LIES IN SHENANDOAH NATIONAL PARK.

white landowners, relationships across the divide could be surprisingly complex. "My great-grandmother was born in 1876 and her middle name was Morgan," said White. "She was named after the man who had owned the family as slaves, and it was his widow who sold them their property after they were freed. So the relationships were not always what you would expect."

Along with the right to go when and where they wanted, the newly freed people wanted an education. It had been illegal to teach a slave in Virginia to read and write, so the demand was great. Even before the government began organizing schools for African Americans, Sarah Steer, one of the brave young Quaker women who had published a pro-Union paper, the *Waterford News*, in Loudoun County during the war, had begun teaching in Waterford in her own yard. Almost half the students at her school, which was formalized as the Second Street School in 1867, were older than 16. Other "freedman's schools" opened across the Piedmont in those years, although some had an unfriendly reception. In Warrenton, a Massachusetts woman named Fannie Wood had opened the Whittier School (named in honor of Quaker and abolitionist John Greenleaf Whittier) in 1866. She soon received a letter

OLD STORER COLLEGE, A FORMER black institution for higher learning in Harpers Ferry, today serves as the communications headquarters for the National Park Service. As the historic marker explains, it was here in August 1906 that the first meeting of the Niagara Movement was held on American soil. Spearheaded by famed black leader W. E. B. Du Bois, the organization developed into a manifestaion of the civil rights movement, as well as the National Association for the Advancement of Colored People (NAACP).

from "Negroeville, VA," stating, "We the young men of this town think you are a disgrace to decent society and therefore wish you to leave this town before the first of March and if you don't there will be violence used to make you comply to this request." Undeterred, she taught on, with a Union Army officer who had lost an arm at Fredericksburg taking the night classes for young adults.

Even more impressive than the efforts of northern philanthropists was the work of African-American heroes such as Jennie Dean, founder of the Manassas Industrial School. Born a slave in 1852 in Prince William County, Dean spent part of her childhood within earshot of the great battles at Manassas. Right after the war her father, who himself learned to read and write in defiance of the law, had just managed to buy his own farm a few miles away when he died. To pay the mortgage and keep the farm—as well as send her younger sister to school—Dean took the rebuilt railroad into Washington and found work as a maid. She herself had received a smattering of education at an elementary school set up by the Freedman's Bureau. The bureau had been established in 1865 to help former slaves, but by the 1880s it had been abolished and public education for African Americans was fading along with other Reconstruction efforts. The public school in Manassas was for white children only.

Dean, who had already organized a Sunday school and a church, set out to raise the money for a school that would teach young African Americans a trade. Not only did she tap a wide network of wealthy and influential whites, including Andrew Carnegie and Edward Everett (the man who spoke before Lincoln at Gettysburg), she also insisted that the local African-American communities contribute. She herself pitched in her savings of $60 as part of the down payment for the school property. In 1892 she organized a Fourth of July picnic for the entire county, raising a further $75. By 1894 she had raised $1,400, and the school finally opened. The days when black and white children could be educated together at public expense in the South were, of course, still far in the future, and African Americans continued to depend on their own efforts. Booker T. Washington, for example, talked Julius Rosenwald, president of Sears, Roebuck, and Company, into matching funds raised by local communities for the Rosenwald schools scattered through the Piedmont and the rest of the South.

"BIRDS SHOULD BE SAVED FOR UTILITARIAN REASONS; AND, MOREOVER, THEY SHOULD BE SAVED BECAUSE OF REASONS UNCONNECTED WITH DOLLARS AND CENTS. A GROVE OF GIANT REDWOODS OR SEQUOIAS SHOULD BE KEPT JUST AS WE KEEP A GREAT AND BEAUTIFUL CATHEDRAL."

—Theodore Roosevelt, U.S. President

CLARA BARTON, REVERED AS THE
Civil War's angel of the battlefield and later
as the founder of the American Red Cross,
dedicated her life to delivering supplies
to soldiers during the Civil War, and afterward to bringing relief worldwide to people
in times of war and natural disaster.

WHILE AFRICAN AMERICANS HAD BEEN LIBERATED BY the Civil War, those turbulent years had also had a huge effect on women. Just as the battlefields of the Piedmont and surrounding region had seen the first effects of modern industrialized warfare, so women for the first time had been enlisted as necessary contributors to the war machines of both sides. Clara Barton, for one, the Patent Office's first female clerk, who began organizing medical services for the Union Army in 1861 and whose sleeve had been nicked by a sniper's bullet at Antietam, was not prepared to retire into obscurity after the war.

As the conflict ended, Barton, whose "rules of action" were "unconcern for what cannot be helped" and "control under pressure," devoted her energies to tracing the fates of the tens of thousands of men listed as "missing" in the casualty reports, including the 13,000 nameless dead at the Confederate Prisoner of War camp at Andersonville, Georgia. In 1869, exhausted, she took a vacation in Europe. There she discovered the International Red Cross, founded a few years earlier and devoted to providing humanitarian services impartially to all victims during wartime under a flag of neutrality. Returning home, she determined to import the organization to the United States. The government was reluctant to accept the notion that the country would ever again be involved in large-scale armed conflict. But in 1881, after extensive lobbying by Barton, the government finally recognized the American Red Cross.

Another of Barton's interests was less successful, at least while she was alive (she died in 1912). Like many women who had been active during the Civil War, she saw no reason why women should be denied the vote. During the war she had written: "I most devoutly wish that intellect, education and moral worth decided a voter's privileges and not sex, or money or land or any other unintelligent principle." Now she lent her support to the growing movement to gain women the right to vote. "Soldiers!" she would tell veterans groups, "I have worked for you and I ask you, now, one and all, that you consider the wants of my people.... God only knows, women were your friends in time of peril and you should be [theirs] now."

Barton's stand against taxation without representation for wom-en was not a novel one. Hannah Lee Corbin, sister of the Revo-lutionary War hero Richard Henry Lee, had complained to her brother about having to pay taxes when she had no say in making

CLARA BARTON'S HOME, in the Washington, D.C., suburb of Glen Echo, Maryland, is today a national historic site. In 1897, Barton moved back to the Washington, D.C., area, after having founded the American Red Cross in 1881 and having traveled widely to establish it. Under her leadership, the organization's early work included assisting victims in the 1882 and 1884 floods of the Mississippi and Ohio Rivers, in the 1886 Texas famine, in Florida's yellow fever epidemic in 1887, and in the 1889 Johnstown flood in Pennsylvania. In 1898, Red Cross workers made their first foray into armed conflict, aiding victims in the Spanish-American War.

In Glen Echo, Barton turned a warehouse into Red Cross national headquarters. Her home there, its remodeled parlor showcased above, remained her permanent residence until her death in 1912. The parlor contains her piano and portrait, along with the American and Red Cross flags. In addition to her deep commitment to the Red Cross, Barton was active in the woman suffrage movement, working closely with Susan B. Anthony and Lucy Stone. She also founded the National First Aid Society in 1904. By the time of her death at age 83, she had become America's most decorated woman, having received the Iron Cross, the Cross of Imperial Russia, and the International Red Cross Medal.

As a young woman, Barton had listened to advice from her dying father and had lived by it: "As a patriot he had me serve my country with all I had ... he had me seek and comfort the afflicted everywhere." Barton's example continues to inspire young and old alike, both in America and around the globe. Her words resonate today: "An institution or reform movement that is not selfish, must originate in the recognition of some evil that is adding to the sum of human suffering, or in diminishing the sum of happiness."

An online activity, the Clara Barton Interactive Experience *(www.nps.gov/features/clba/feat0001/flash.html)*, helps young people learn about this remarkable woman and allows them to become online Junior Rangers of the National Park Service.

A WORLD WAR II REENACTMENT at former President Dwight D. Eisenhower's Gettysburg farm (white house in left background) takes place every autumn, complete with uniformed soldiers, jeeps, halftracks, and parades. The barn (center background) continues to house cattle as it did during Ike's lifetime. He and Mamie enjoyed their retirement on the historic battlefield site.

laws or choosing the men who made them. (She was ahead of her time in other ways, too. Because married women back then lost all rights to their own property, Corbin refused to remarry after being widowed, instead openly living with her partner.) Now more and more women were asking the same question. Elizabeth Van Lew, for example, had been a Union spy in Richmond during the war, managing an espionage network that reached into Jefferson Davis's household, while she deflected suspicion by pretending to be mad. A social outcast after the war, she paid her taxes every year under protest, always reminding the authorities that she was taxed but not represented. Orra Langhorne, an eloquent journalist who lived in both Lynchburg and Culpeper, was equally passionate about the civil rights of women and blacks, becoming president of the Virginia Suffrage Association in 1893, although one historian describes her "unfailing optimism" as "unfounded." Always eager to expand her horizons, Langhorne enrolled as a college student at the age of 56.

Despite these pioneers, the Piedmont, once the heart of a revolution, was generally conservative as regards the status of women, even in the early years of the 20th century. (Married women in Virginia gained the right to control their own property only in 1877.) That may have been why locals in Fauquier County found one aspect of what became known as the Second Yankee Invasion especially shocking: the sight of women riding astride for the first time.

The "invasion" came in the form of the Orange County Hunt, imported in 1905 by robber baron E. H. Harriman and named for its origin in Orange County, New York. Harriman and a group of fellow foxhunters had decided to move south because development in the Hudson Valley was encroaching on their hunting country. The comparatively empty hills and valleys of the northern Piedmont seemed ideal:Its grasslands had long been famous for the horses bred there, and the U.S. Army maintained its principal remount depot at Front Royal.

The horsemen drawn to the Piedmont were only one variety of outsiders who recognized the unique attractions of the area. In 1905, about the time the Orange County Hunt arrived in The Plains, President Theodore Roosevelt came for the first time to Pine Knot, an unpretentious cabin in the woods of Albemarle County south of Charlottesville. Here the man credited with the creation of our National Park Service took solace and respite away from the White House (he was delayed moving in by having to settle the Russo-Japanese War). When he first visited, he announced to the locals that he was "glad to become a landowner in your community" and began the fashion for presidential retreats that would culminate with the famous Camp David farther north in the Hallowed Ground corridor, in Frederick County, Maryland.

Only a century earlier, it had taken Thomas Jefferson four days and three nights to travel from nearby Monticello to Washington. Roosevelt could make the journey in a day, the last ten miles on horseback. The famously hyperactive President, who relished the "strenuous life," celebrated the shooting of his first and only wild turkey, and pronounced the holiday home, which had been found and bought by his wife, Edith, "the nicest little place of the kind you could imagine."

On that trip Roosevelt also made what is considered the last reliable sighting of a wild passenger pigeon in the United States. Once upon a time these birds had flowed across the skies of the eastern seaboard in multimillion-strong flocks, but by the early 1900s they had been hunted to extinction. Almost a hundred years earlier, James Madison had lamented the wanton destruction of forests in Albemarle County. His call had gone largely unheard, but Roosevelt would take a concern for nature further, making conservation of the landscape official policy and founding the National Park Service. "Birds should be saved for utilitarian reasons; and, moreover, they should be saved because of reasons unconnected with dollars and cents. A grove of giant redwoods or sequoias should be kept just as we keep a great and beautiful cathedral," he wrote later.

Five Presidents later, Herbert Hoover made tracks to the same region, professing equal regard for the beauties and simplicities of nature within the Piedmont. His chosen hideaway, Rapidan Camp, was farther up the Blue Ridge than Pine Knot, chosen for its elevation and adjacency to both Washington, D.C., and to trout. As Hoover explained in a speech in August 1929, fishing was an

READING THE MARSHALL PLAN
from the steps of the Leesburg, Virginia, courthouse, reenactor Tim Jon outlines Gen. George C. Marshall's points for European recovery after World War II. A five-minute walk down the main street leads one to Dodona Manor, which Marshall and his wife called home from 1941 until his death in 1959.

AT DODONA MANOR IN LEESBURG,
a simple desk with typewriter and lamp
marks the spot where George C. Marshall
spent time implementing many of the plans
he developed to ensure the nation's well-
being after World War II, including writing
the Marshall Plan. Also housed here is
the George C. Marshall International
Center, which focuses on his contributions
to modern history and also serves as an
educational center.

"excuse for return to the woods and streams with their retouch of the simpler life of the frontier from which every American springs." The retreat, he said, was a means to escape "the pneumatic hammer of public life."

Among the many acts of individual courage and leadership found along the Journey Through Hallowed Ground, the courage and vision of W. E. B. Du Bois stands tall. In 1906, in an effort build opposition to racial segregation and disenfranchisement as well as to create policies of accommodation and conciliation promoted by African-American leaders, Du Bois convened the meeting that led to the Niagara Movement. It was named for the "mighty current" of change the group wanted to effect and for the location of the first meeting in July 1905 on the Canadian side of Niagara Falls. One story, which cannot be substantiated with primary sources, states that although the planners originally wanted to meet in Buffalo, New York, they were refused accommodation, hence the need to meet in Canada. Their second meeting, the first to be held on U.S. soil, took place at Harpers Ferry, West Virginia, the historic site of John Brown's raid. The three-day gathering, starting on

HITCHCOCK'S
NEW AND
COMPLETE ANALYSIS
OF THE
HOLY BIBLE:
OR, THE WHOLE OF THE
OLD AND NEW TESTAMENTS
ARRANGED ACCORDING TO SUBJECTS
IN TWENTY-SEVEN BOOKS.

ON THE BASIS OF MATTHEW TALBOT, AS IMPROVED WITH INDEXES, TABLES, AND OTHER VALUABLE MATTER BY NATHANIEL WEST, D.D.

Illustrated with Copper Plate Maps, and Engravings.

THE ENGRAVINGS ARE ORIGINAL DRAWINGS BY THE CELEBRATED ARTISTS
AND F. B. CARPENTER

THE HOLY SCRIPTURES

WITH

UNITED PRESB. CHURCH, SCOT

PROMOTE THE BET

CRUDEN'S CO
REVISED BY JOHN EA
THE WHOLE

WORMLEY HUGHES
A likeness of the Preacher Wormley Hughes, great grandfather of Karen Hughes White (right) rests on a copy of the family Bible. Fauquier County has been home to succeeding generations of the family for centuries. Wormley Hughes, whose grandfather worked as a gardener to Jefferson at Monticello, was a preacher to the black community in Fauquier and Loudoun Counties and founded Mt. Zion Baptist Church at Gilbert's Corner.

KAREN HUGHES WHITE

WE TELL THE STORY OF HOW AFRICAN AMERICANS SURVIVED— THEIR ACCOMPLISHMENTS THROUGHOUT HISTORY AND HOW THEY CONTRIBUTED TO THE HISTORY OF THIS COUNTY.

A s director of the Afro-American Historical Association of Fauquier County, which exhibits African-American history and provides a library of culture, heritage, and a genealogy, Karen Hughes White has unearthed records of African-American families and their contributions to our American heritage.

"We tell the story of how African Americans survived—their accomplishments throughout history and how they contributed to the history of this county. As an African American I have learned how my ancestors survived. Today, I learn from their character, their strengths and from their weaknesses. It may not all be a pleasant history, but it's still our history and we can certainly learn from it. I realize that I am very much a mixed child of Virginia, and I say that word 'mixed' because I am descended from so many different people, in different walks of life, and am predominantly African American.

"My family has been in Virginia for generations, dating at least to their lives at Monticello. On my father's side, I'm descended

Karen Hughes White, Afro-American Historical Association

from Betty Brown, the daughter of Elizabeth Hemmings. Her son was Wormley Hughes, the gardener at Monticello, and his son, Robert, was the preacher at Union Run. My great-grandfather, also named Wormley Hughes, first settled in Fauquier County after the Civil War. At that time, my mother's family lived in Fauquier County as free people from before the Civil War.

"I am open to accept who I am. The only way I can do that is by learning from and preserving history itself. I became familiar with my family's history by doing genealogical research. In this rigorous endeavour, one must learn the laws that governed one's ancestors in order to know where to look for their records.

"From the records of how people escaped slavery, to the stories of the people that enslaved them, you need to look at the whole picture to understand history. By looking at the entire picture, you begin to understand the actual character of those people involved. If you understand them, you understand a little bit more about the treatment of African Americans, about their contributions to our country and about ourselves."

KAREN HUGHES WHITE STROLLS

past the schoolhouse near Marshall, Virginia, which she attended during grade school. Long abandoned and in disrepair, the building was heated by a single stove, for which White remembers stacking wood. Her family's long history in this part of the Piedmont provides plenty of background for her work as director of the Afro-American Historical Association of Fauquier County.

August 15, 1906, at the campus of Storer College, discussed how to secure for African Americans the civil rights espoused by Jefferson as part of our American ideals. The meeting was later described by Du Bois as "one of the greatest meetings that American Negroes ever held." Attendees, inspired by the selfless acts of those who went before them, walked from Storer College to the nearby Murphy family farm, site of the historic fort where John Brown's quest to free four million enslaved blacks reached its bloody climax. Once there they removed their shoes and socks to honor the hallowed ground and participated in a ceremony of remembrance.

The decision to hold this first American meeting at Harpers Ferry was intentionally symbolic. The clear tie to John Brown, who in 1859 led the raid against slavery on this site, inspired the new generation of leaders to forge ahead in pursuit of their ideals. The choice of Storer College was also appropriate: the Freewill Baptists had opened it in 1867 as a mission school to educate "all regardless of sex, race or religion." As a result, for more than 25 years Storer was the only school in West Virginia to offer African Americans an education beyond the primary level. This seminal meeting is considered by many to have been the beginning of the modern-day civil rights movement, since those present would help launch the NAACP a few years later.

THE EARLIEST SETTLERS HAD MADE THEIR WAY ACROSS THE Piedmont to the mountains in the first part of the 18th century. Although frontier settlement soon moved farther west into the Shenandoah Valley and beyond, many pioneers stayed on the Blue Ridge. Among other advantages, the mountain landscape offered the plentiful harvest of the American chestnut trees that carpeted the mountainside, making up probably one in every four of the trees in the entire Appalachian Mountains chain. Not only magnificent in themselves, they were an economic boon for the people who lived in their shade. The sweet nuts that dropped in the fall were a source of food both for humans and their hogs, which could maintain themselves cost-free for half the year by being left to roam in the woods. The fast-growing, straight-grained wood was easy to saw and split. Because it was rich in tannins, it did not rot and was therefore highly prized for everything from furniture to telephone poles, and the tannins extracted from it were in demand for tanning leather. However, a devastating blight that first appeared in the early years of the 20th century spread inexorably across the eastern seaboard. By the early 1930s, most of the Blue Ridge chestnuts were gone. Soon, the hundreds of families who had lived among them would be gone too, as the area had been selected as suitable for a national park.

THE CONCEPT OF A "SHENANDOAH NATIONAL PARK" WAS heartily endorsed by some in the community, who correctly calculated that it would be a major tourist draw. In the process, those who lived within the designated park boundaries were belittled as primitive "native people" living in conditions "representing about the limit of destitution at which human life could be sustained." In reality, the people concerned may not have been rich, but most were happy with their way of life and were unwilling, as one of them wrote to President Hoover, "to part with our homes to help a small part of our population to get their hands into tourists' pockets."

Shenandoah National Park was officially inaugurated by President Franklin Roosevelt in July 1936, although the wheelchair-bound Roosevelt found Hoover's Rapidan Camp unsuitable. He instead selected his own Shangri La in Maryland's Catoctin Mountains, the site that later became famous as Camp David. Still, he had a deep fascination with Thomas Jefferson and loved to spend time at Monticello. FDR often visited his good friend and longtime military aide, Edwin "Pa" Watson, at Kenwood, a comfortable retreat almost next door to his predecessor's mountaintop home. It was here that he waited in the fateful days of June 1944, before returning to Washington as Allied forces embarked for Normandy and the D-Day invasion.

Two men intimately connected to that invasion, Gens. George Marshall and Dwight Eisenhower, were also drawn to this region. Marshall, the military statesman whom Winston Churchill called "the organizer of victory" in World War II, found his retreat at Dodona, a country home in Leesburg, Virginia. He called it his one and only home, "after 41 years of wandering." Here the only American to serve as U.S. Army chief of staff, secretary of defense, secretary of state, and president of the American Red Cross pondered the development of his program (the Marshall Plan), for postwar European reconstruction. Drawing on the knowledge of those who lived in the Hallowed Ground region and served before him, Marshall personified the ideals of serving one's country. Just as American Revolutionary soldiers sought to take revenge on their Hessian prisoners of war, acts thwarted by General Washington's decision to treat the captives civilly, many throughout the world wanted to punish Germany following World War II. Yet Marshall believed that to support and stabilize Europe, a conciliatory approach to reconstruction was necessary. His plan, delivered at a Harvard University commencement, resulted in his becoming a Nobel laureate and led the world to share these uniquely American ideals.

Eisenhower had come to know the Gettysburg landscape at the end of World War I when serving at the Army's tank training school, which conducted its exercises on the site of Pickett's Charge. In 1950 he bought a farm on the edge of the battlefield. During his

first term as President, he and his wife, Mamie, renovated this home and eventually were able to enjoy it with friends and family over weekends and holidays. It is reported that the President, an avid sportsman, enjoyed playing golf at the Gettysburg Country Club and shooting skeet at his shooting range. After 45 years' service to the country, the Eisenhowers retired to the farm in 1961. During the ensuing eight years, the former President worked from his Gettysburg College office and served as an elder statesman, advising Presidents and meeting world leaders. In 1967 the Eisenhowers donated their home and farm to the National Park Service.

The stories of the known and the unknown throughout this region, each of whom found sustenance, inspiration, and courage to serve others, are reminders that our American ideals have been built, generation after generation, through individual acts of courage and selflessness.

THEODORE ROOSEVELT'S RETREAT,
Pine Knot, near Keene, Virginia, is 20 miles south of Monticello on Route 20. This vacation home for the President; his wife, Edith; and their brood of children was a respite that allowed the nonstop go-getter Teddy—along with his friend, the nature writer John Burroughs—to indulge a passion for nature. Together they identified 75 different bird species in the forest around Pine Knot.

OATLANDS PLANTATION
Oatlands Plantation, just south of Leesburg, Virginia, is the second property ever donated to the National Trust for Historic Preservation. Currently owned and operated by the organization, the 19th-century property pays for its own maintenance by hosting various events, such as steeplechases, dog shows, weddings and needlework and art exhibits.

OATLANDS PLANTATION
The colorful autumn tree-lined drive at Oatlands Plantation near Leesburg, Virginia, looks onto its front field. The 1,200-acre plantation succeeds in preserving the soul of the surrounding community.

The Living Land

The Living Land

"THE RAVAGES OF WAR HAVE NOT BEEN ABLE TO DESTROY THE BEAUTIES OF NATURE—THE VERDURE IS CHARMING, THE TREES MAGNIFICENT, THE COUNTRY UNDULATING, AND THE BLUE RIDGE MOUNTAINS FORM THE BACKGROUND." —COL. ARTHUR FREEMANTLE, JUNE 21, 1863

As Pulitzer Prize-winning historian David McCullough observed about the Journey Through Hallowed Ground region, "[T]his is the ground of our Founding Fathers. These are landscapes that speak volumes—small towns, churches, fields, mountains, creeks and rivers with names such as Bull Run and Rappahannock. They are the real thing, and what shame we will bring on ourselves if we destroy them." The communities

that form the backbone of this region have borne generations of exceptional citizens who strove, each in his or her own way, for the greater good of their communities, their states, and our country.

These communities—Charlottesville, Orange, Madison, Culpeper, Fauquier, Prince William, Spotsylvania, Loudoun, Harpers Ferry, Frederick, and Adams County, to name but a few—stand today not only as a touchstone of the ideals of our American heritage, but also by deliberate effort as vibrant centers for commerce and entertainment utilizing 18th- and 19th-century historic structures.

The evolution of these thriving towns has been nothing short of remarkable. Consider the fate of so many other communities across the country. Rural and historic downtowns were literally torn down in the 1970s as Main Street shops were shuttered, unable to compete with the new retail and business center developments. Faced with the loss of these culturally and historically significant downtowns, the National Trust for Historic Preservation began the innovative Main Street Program more than 25 years ago. "The Main Street Program developed a comprehensive approach for older downtowns and commercial districts to revitalize themselves in the face of growing competition from regional malls," said Peter Brink, senior vice president, Programs, National Trust for Historic Preservation. This locally driven program consists of a four-pronged approach combining organization, design, marketing, and economic restructuring. Along the historic corridor, the elected, business, and volunteer leaders of 16 communities have worked with the National Trust Main Street Program to sustain the irreplaceable ingredients that create these lively, thriving towns, which continue to attract new and innovative entrepreneurs. According to Brink, as of 2006, more than 2,000 communities had utilized the Main Street Program, attracting over $41 billion in reinvestment and a net gain of more than 77,000 new businesses.

Culpeper, Virginia, for example, a town first surveyed by young George Washington, has structures predating the 1749 establishment of Culpeper County. In one of these structures,

HORSES DRAW PERIOD-COSTUMED RIDERS IN UPPERVILLE, VIRGINIA.

a man named John Yarnall, decided to open an innovative restaurant called It's About Thyme in 1995. The restaurant offers
"European country dining" with menu items such as ceviche—a
rarity for that place and time. Customers flocked to the restaurant
not just for the food, but for the experience of dining in an atmospheric historic structure. Yarnall's success spawned a new kind
of revitalization.

Soon, a store selling Aboriginal Australian blouses and Guatema-
lan dolls opened a few doors down, then an art gallery appeared,
and then the venerable Hazel River Inn got a face-lift. These entrepreneurs were dedicated to maintaining the historic vibrancy of a
region where Founding Fathers had formulated the nation's earliest
ideals, and where civil war had raged in challenge and in support
of those ideals. The town officials sought and received a grant to
make over the historic train station, which had ferried Confederate and Union troops in and out of town during the Civil War,

"THANKS TO THE
EASEMENT, THIS
LANDSCAPE IS
PRESERVED
FOREVER."

—*Cliff Miller,
fifth-generation
family farmer in
Rappahannock
County, Virginia*

and today this masterpiece serves as a visitor center for all train and pedestrian travelers. A specialty store selling locally produced food, a refurbished movie theater, and other attractions followed not long after, all in tasteful keeping with the cultural fabric of the community. By 2007, downtown Culpeper had revived to the point that reports of its compelling historic restoration were published in newspapers in Sweden.

Culpeper is not alone in the success of its historic downtown area. A recent PBS television special spotlighted the rich cluster of cultural attractions along Route 15 in Hallowed Ground territory, with a focus on the vibrancy of the 16 historic Main Street communities: Gettysburg, Pennsylvania; Harpers Ferry, West Virginia; Frederick, Mount Airy, Thurmont, and Brunswick, Maryland; and Leesburg, Hamilton, Hillsboro, Purcellville, Middleburg, Warrenton, Culpeper, Orange, Gordonsville, and Charlottesville, Virginia. Each of these communities has worked to sustain its character. A stroll down the streets of any one of these towns is anything but dull. Artist galleries fill former warehouses in Orange, Virginia. The original pre-Revolutionary City Hall in Frederick, Maryland, houses a magnificent restaurant and is surrounded by cyber cafés, coffee houses, antique markets, and thriving theaters. Just down the road in Loudoun County, Virginia, the towns of Purcellville and Middleburg pulse with innovative cafés, unique clothing shops, international cuisine, and organic farm markets.

Leesburg, the county seat of Loudoun County, Virginia, was called "George Town," after the reigning English monarch, King George II, until 1758, when the name was changed to Leesburg, in honor of the influential Lee family of Virginia. It was here that colonial farmers and city dwellers gathered in the courthouse and taverns to discuss taxes and the king. The same buildings survive to host similar discussions among business luncheons and social gatherings today. The same Old Carolina Road along which General Lafayette paraded into this town in 1825 now welcomes community festivals and parades that celebrate the past and current culture of the area. Throughout the historic corridor, stately old homes and mansions have been preserved as inns and bed-and-breakfasts. Specialty shops and local festivals offer rare shopping experiences ranging from chic to casual in elegant historic structures.

Combined, these efforts to revitalize the historic elements of each community have created special places that tell the stories of our past even as they incubate new history. The remarkable public and private sector efforts to which the leaders of these communities have committed themselves in order to sustain their hometowns have not gone unnoticed. Gettysburg, Pennsylvania; Frederick Maryland; and Leesburg and Warrenton in Virginia have each been designated a Preserve America Community by the President's Advisory Council on Historic Preservation.

THE HISTORIC STRUCTURES ARE NOT THE ONLY ESSENTIAL component of these communities. The farmland between and within these historic towns forms part of the cultural fabric of these areas. Decades ago, threatened by climbing real estate taxes,

CATE MAGENNIS WYATT, founder and president of the Journey Through Hallowed Ground Partnership, launches two participants to join others on their way down to Ball's Bluff from White's Ferry. As participants in the Extreme Journey Through Hallowed Ground, a summer school educational outreach program for middle school youngsters, these students travel highlights of the 175-mile route by foot, canoe, and bicycle for a two-week period. Aided by iPods and digital cameras, they absorb the rich history of the region, and at the end of the journey, create their own presentations of the experience. High schoolers participate in Extreme Journey High School Camp, a two-week residential leadership immersion program co-sponsored by the University of Virginia Summer Enrichment Program.

A PRODUCTIVE HUNT
Riders and mounts participate in a fox hunt in Rappahannock County, Virginia. Conservation easements link farms together so that the hunt can continue. In return, owners receive a tax break. Moreover, the land is preserved. These events also lure horse enthusiasts, fueling one of the major industries of the region.

farmers turned to lawmakers for relief. State assemblies enacted programs in the 1970s to give farmers tax credits in exchange for removing the development rights from their farms. Easements became a means by which each landowner could donate all rights to develop the land to an approved entity, and while not receiving the full financial benefit of a sale, could realize a reasonable tax benefit.

Among the more important sites benefited by the easement program is Jefferson's own Monticello. Over the years, the Thomas Jefferson Foundation, the private non-profit corporation that owns and operates Monticello, has acquired about half of the 5,000 acres Jefferson once owned. More recently, it has placed conservation easements on his birthplace estate (215 acres) as well as his Home Farm (1,060 acres). The latter transaction also involved the sale of tax credits, and the proceeds were used to help pay down the debt for the purchase of Montalto (330 acres), which Jefferson owned

ACOLYTES PROCESS TO A SERVICE

at Grace Episcopal Church in The Plains, Virginia. The church dates to the 1800s, built during a period in Virginia's heritage when any religious practice other than Anglicanism was forbidden. The church today is a community hub full of traditions, including a concert series and regional art shows.

and which dominated his views to the west. Now visitors have the opportunity to experience the sweeping views from Monticello much as Jefferson did. Likewise, the Civil War Preservation Trust has spent two decades working to protect Civil War battlefields throughout the country, and has conserved more than 5,000 acres within Hallowed Ground region alone. According to Jim Lighthizer, president of the Civil War Preservation Trust, "The easement tax credit is a vital tool and Virginia's program is the best program in America. It allows us to move quickly to purchase critical sites and then allows us to sell our credits on the open market. In Maryland, the program is more limited, with a capped state income tax credit, but this, too, is helpful."

From small beginnings, easements have emerged as one of the most successful land conservation programs in American history, and not surprisingly, the leading landowners in the country for placing land in easement are those within the Hallowed Ground corridor, where the historical and cultural value of the land is so great. In the Virginia portion of the corridor, the amount of land preserved in this fashion has grown to no less than 300,000 acres. In Fauquier County, 72,000 acres of the farmland is under easement. In Frederick County, Maryland's leading county for agriculture, some 20,000 acres are under easement as of the end of 2007, while Adams County in Pennsylvania, scene of the epochal 1863 Gettysburg campaign, has preserved 11,600 acres.

EASEMENTS NOT ONLY ATTRACT THE WEALTHY DONORS intrigued by those tax benefits but also allow family farmers to stay in business and pass farmland on to their children without ruinous estate taxes. To see a working farm under easement one need go no farther than Mount Vernon Farm, just outside Sperryville in Rappahannock County, Virginia. Owner Cliff Miller is the fifth generation of his family to farm this land since his great-great-great-grandfather arrived here in 1827. "They raised cattle and other livestock organically, like me," he laughed, looking at some of his herd of 115 Black Angus cattle grazing contentedly on the valley bottom next to the Thornton River. The animals occupy 250 acres of the farm's 850 acres. In fact, all but 200 acres surrounding the town of Sperryville is under a conservation easement. "Thanks to the easement, this landscape is preserved forever," said Miller with satisfaction, gazing across the valley to the mounting Blue Ridge foothills. Down below

"THEY STOP AND SEE THE DISPLAY OF ALL OUR FRUIT AND VEGETABLES, AND THEY ASK, 'WHERE DOES ALL THIS COME FROM?' AND I TELL THEM, 'RIGHT HERE.'"

—*Robert Black, third-generation farmer and co-owner of Catoctin Mountain Orchard*

CATTLE COUNTRY
A snowy day on a cattle farm near Broad Run, three miles east of
The Plains, Virginia, is a common scene in this cattle-farming area.
Large farms such as this one keep the land open and protect the
landscape's character.

was the road from Culpeper to Front Royal that Arthur Freemantle, an English colonel, rode on June 21, 1863, on his way to meet up with the Confederate Army. Freemantle had noted in his diary about this precise spot that "the ravages of war have not been able to destroy the beauties of nature—the verdure is charming, the trees magnificent, the country undulating, and the Blue Ridge mountains form the background."

Miller is an evangelist for methods of food production that have a lot more in common with his ancestors' techniques than recent mainstream practice but that may nonetheless be the salvation of agriculture within this country. Mainstream beef cattle production consists of rearing calves for a season, then selling them to a feedlot somewhere in the Midwest, where they are fattened up on corn before slaughter. "Since cattle aren't naturally suited to eating grain, they have to be fed antibiotics to get over the effects of the corn," he explained, pointing out that grass-fed beef is far richer in vital antioxidants and vitamins. He decried the practice of putting a grass-fed animal on a grain diet for a few weeks before slaughter. "Any grain at all diminshes the health benefits of grass feeding."

In essence, Miller's alternative to conventional livestock farming methods consists of raising the animals entirely on fresh grass (even eliminating hay almost entirely from their winter diet), using as little fossil fuel as possible—haymaking consumes a lot of tractor fuel—and confining almost the entire operation to the farm. "My cattle go to be butchered in Fauquier 45 minutes away, which is too far," he said regretfully. Finally, he insists on selling his meat locally, minimizing the energy cost of shipment and delivery. "I get emails from people in California wanting to buy my beef and I tell them there are plenty of fine grass-fed farms near them and they should shop there." He either sells his cuts of meat directly from the store at the farm, or otherwise operates through local buyers' clubs.

There is more to raising animals on grass than simply letting them loose in a field. Miller pointed to the cattle feeding on the valley bottom. "See how they're all in a line? That's because they're

CABERNET SAUVIGNON GRAPES (opposite, top) ripen on vines at the Boxwood Winery near Middleburg, Virginia. Grapes and wine are one of the biggest new clean industries in the state, producing a value added agriculture that does not deplete the soil. Coming over Ashby's Gap from Winchester to Upperville, a view of Paris Valley (below) remains much as it was when the territory was still undiscovered by Europeans. Rumor has it that on a clear day one can view all the way to Charlottesville.

ANTICIPATING THE HUNT
An eager beagle sticks his nose out from the back of a pickup truck. The late Mrs. Eve Fout (opposite) stands ready to gather youngsters together for her Sunday fox hunt, as part of an educational outreach program.

EVE FOUT

**WE HAVE TO DO IT,
AND WE WILL FIGURE OUT
HOW WE WILL DO IT ALONG THE WAY.**

The term irreplaceable should rarely be used, but it is descriptive of the contributions and the leadership of Eve Fout, who passed away December 5, 2007. Longtime chair of the Piedmont Environmental Council, Fout was energized by her deep connection to the Piedmont. She grew up in Fauquier County, Virginia, where she moved with her parents at the age of ten and participated zealously in the county's equestrian traditions and conservation ethic. A formidable horsewoman, Fout was the first female trainer to saddle the winner of the Virginia Gold Cup, Moon Rock, in 1964. She rode until just before her death; in fact, in October 2007, she won the North American Field Hunter Championship. Two of her children inherited their mother's passion for horses: her son, a renowned equestrian trainer one daughter, an Olympic equestrian rider.

Fout felt compelled to pass the working landscape she supported and sustained on to future generations. She often encouraged people with her characteristically

Eve Fout, Piedmont
Environmental Council

vigorous advice: "You need to be a self-starter and get on with it!"

Fout was one of the first to recognize the potential of voluntary, private land conservation easements and ultimately would spearhead one of the most successful conservation movements in America. She helped to conserve thousands of acres of private land in the Piedmont, preserving some of the nation's most precious historic, cultural, and scenic resources.

When confronted with a seemingly insurmountable challenge, she often said, "We have to do it, and we will figure out how we will do it along the way." She was fearless, passionate, and a steadfast visionary for the Journey Through Hallowed Ground Partnership, her community and the entire state of Virginia. Fout has left a lasting legacy in her work as chair of the Piedmont Environmental Council, trustee of Scenic Virginia, and supporter of the Middleburg-Orange County Pony Club, which introduces young children to the world of equestrian sports. We all benefit from her vision, kindness, generosity and leadership.

between two electric fences—solar powered—that we move every day." Continually moving the cattle means they crop the grass evenly, and their manure is scattered, thus eliminating the need for a mechanical manure spreader. Even more important, the cattle are followed into the field by sheep. "Rotating different animals through the pasture is essential," said Miller, delving into some very specific explanations of the different kinds of worms affecting cows, and how putting sheep on the same pasture, with careful monitoring, deals with the problem more effectively than chemical dewormers. His Internet-based distribution methods are similarly more complicated for the individual farmer than the industrial system of grain-reliant feedlots and meatpacking plants. "A lot of guys don't want to be bothered by that," he said, "but with the cost of gas and corn going up all the time, the old way is getting very expensive."

As farming becomes increasingly skilled, farmers not only produce better quality yields with more environmentally sustainable

SPERRYVILLE MARKET, ON HIGHWAY 211 heading up to Skyland Drive and the Hoover Cabin, is a roadside attraction offering local delicacies, such as apple butter, Virginia ham, and bacon. Another example of added value farming, it takes nothing from the land and also provides sales to tourists.

methods, but they also devise new ways of delivering their products—whether grass-fed beef or farm-fresh produce—to their customers. Members of a remarkably humble yet important industry for national sustenance, fruit growers occupy a vibrant 20-mile-long "fruit belt" stretching south from Adams County, Pennsylvania. Through the Revolutionary War, the Civil War, and straight on through World War II, the area flourished and provided food for troops and citizens. Today, the fruit belt is a concentrated area of fruit farms, with pick-your-own orchards and fields, festivals, and fruit stands selling prepared foods made from ripe yields. The trip through these orchards and the breathtaking beauty of this region are reasons enough to take a drive through the corridor, but imagine biting into a crisp, juicy apple just plucked off its tree in early fall; the taste is irresistible.

In Thurmont, Maryland, Catoctin Mountain Orchard welcomes fruit pickers and shoppers to its homey market, as well as offering gift-basket deliveries and online sales. Farther down the road, in Waterford, Virginia, organic farming entrepreneurs Zach Lester and Georgia O'Neal continue a long tradition of farming in this region, based on innovations made hundreds of years ago. In the early 1780s, in his *Notes on the State of Virginia*, Jefferson described

A YOUNG BOY MAKES A SELECTION AT the Adams County, Pennsylvania, annual Apple Festival. Between 20,000 and 30,000 people attend the two-weekend event in October just 20 miles north of Gettysburg in Arendtville. Several events—including car shows and the selling of the area delicacy, funnel cakes, as well as apple butter—add to the festival's fun.

THE FALL GOLD CUP
In fall 2007, the purse for the main race out of ten at this yearly event is a whopping $100,000. The races, held at Great Meadow in The Plains, Virginia, vary from steeplechase to flat ground. A Spring Gold Cup offers a chief purse of $50,000.

BUCOLIC SCENES OF FARMLAND
near Upperville, Virginia (opposite), attest
to the fact that taking part in land easement
helps to preserve the landscape through
agriculture. Farming helps to maintain the
beauty of the landscape.

the farming methods of the Waterford farmers, particularly their newly developed methods to ensure the health of their soils by lyming the fields. This technique continues to result in an ample harvest, as it did in Jefferson's time. Lester and O'Neal operate and run their organic farm based on this and other useful local traditions, growing herbs, vegetables and flowers for direct marketing in the Washington, D.C., area. Customers not only get to enjoy fresh produce but also have the satisfaction of supporting a local agricultural enterprise.

MANY OF THESE FAMILY-RUN BUSINESSES ARE ABLE TO operate profitably as a result of maintaining vigilance over operating costs, keeping staffs lean, and adhering to cost-effective measures, such as minimizing distribution costs. Robert Black, Catoctin Mountain Orchard's co-owner along with his sister, Pat, said, "If I had to deal with a wholesaler, I'd have to sell the farm." The Blacks are currently training their fourth generation to run the family farm. For the most part, the Blacks customers come to them, turning off the historic corridor's Route 15, about 18 miles north of Frederick, Maryland. During the Revolutionary War, this farm's great oak trees were harvested and burned to create the charcoal used down the road at Catoctin Furnace to make cannonballs. During the Civil War, Lee drew his troops to this area to reap the benefits of the flourishing harvest. Much later, during World War II, Robert Black remembers that acres and acres of peach orchards were planted along the hillsides to help feed the Allied troops. Today, the tradition continues.

"They stop and see the display of all our fruit and vegetables, and they ask, 'Where does all this come from?' and I tell them, 'Right here.'" The Blacks are practicing "agro-tourism," a concept that is familiar in parts of Europe, where travelers are used to staying or at least shopping at working farms, but less familiar in the United States. At Catoctin Mountain Orchard, customers can pick their own fruit or cut their own flowers and leave with a sense that they have actually touched nature, seen exactly where their food was grown, and understood a bit about how it was grown. Other farmers have embraced the concept of agritourism as well. Black pays particular gentlemanly tribute to Martha Hauver at Pryor's Orchard not far away: "I tell her she's a better grower than I am."

CHERRY PICKERS
Farmer Robert Black's grandchildren harvest cherries, the result of successful cross-pollination. The Blacks have been farming this land for generations,
with knowledge passed from parents to children.

CATOCTIN MT. ORCHARD
1½ MILES NORTH OF
THURMONT, MD. 21788
PHONE 301-271-2737

ROBERT BLACK

**PEOPLE WANT TO SUPPORT THE LOCAL FARMERS.
THAT'S IMPORTANT, BECAUSE IF YOU DON'T SUPPORT THE
LOCAL FARMERS, LOCAL FARMERS WON'T BE HERE.**

obert Black is the co-owner of Catoctin Mountain Orchard at Thurmont, Maryland, on Route 15. All the fruit and produce he sells are grown there on his 125-acre orchard. A skilled businessman from a long line of successful entrepreneurs, he is the second generation of Blacks to till this soil. He is proud that both his children and grandchildren are actively engaged in continuing the Black farming legacy, participating in the rich agricultural industry of this region.

"Back in 1948, Charlie Dunbar, who was the extension agent for the University of Maryland, said to my father, 'I think you should build a market, and put out the best you can put out. Don't put the bad junk in the bottom of the box.' We put out a quality product with a fair price on it and the rest is history.

"We used to sell wholesale, but it just kept tapering off. As we got more retail customers, instead of us delivering to them, they would come to us, and they would tell other folks and more folks would come.

Robert Black, co-owner of
Catoctin Mountain Orchard

"We are encouraging folks to walk around through the orchard and see what we're doing, because even with all the produce and all the fruit that we grow, there are people who walk in our door that apparently don't look up at the hill and see all these trees. They say, 'Where's all this fruit coming from?' I say 'Go out the door, walk up 500 feet.' And when they do, their mouths will drop, they'll say, 'Gosh, they're growing it all here!' I do think people are more concerned, more so now than ever, about where their fruit is from. We get a lot of folks stopping by on their way home from work to buy apples, peaches, berries, good-quality food to take back home for their families. People want to support the local farmers. That's important, because if you don't support the local farmers, local farmers won't be here.

"Access to Route 15 is what's going to keep this farm going. Right now, it's very convenient for folks to get off the road and stretch their legs and visit with us since [Catoctin Mountain Orchard] is very visible, right off Route 15. I can handle pretty much any insect, disease, drought, or hailstorms, but I've got to have that access."

CHAPTER 5 THE LIVING LAND 193

The ties of these landowners to the land run deep. This fertile swath most likely nurtured the crops of ancient Native Americans. Later, settlers who farmed the land held it dear as their means to freedom from British tyranny.

As the previous land stewards learned, success requires a lot of careful attention to detail over the years, not to mention a readiness to innovate. For example, Black avoids spraying with pesticides by utilizing integrated pest management, employing "the good bugs to eat the bad bugs." In addition, the entire Black farm is irrigated by a drip feed system, originally installed when Black's father, Harry, noticed that the fruit flourished during a summer of regular rains. The system is composed of miles of tubing snaking along the beds. Driven by small electric pumps, the water dribbles out of holes every 24 inches along the tubes. "That means we don't waste a lot of water spraying. It's probably cut our water use by a third, and we're using a quarter of the horsepower we used to need for powering the hoses." Thanks to this system and the four irrigation ponds dug on the farm years ago, Catoctin Mountain Orchard was able to weather the severe summer drought of 2007 with equanimity. Meanwhile, as Black noted cheerfully, his apple-growing competitors 3,000 miles

A VARIETY OF GOODS IS OFFERED at Home Farm, a traditional butcher and grazier at 1 Washington Street in Middleburg. The business is "Certified Humane," as the sign attests, which means that all animals are raised in the absence of cruel methods. In addition, because all of the goods are locally grown, less fuel is wasted in transport, the consumers get fresher food, and the farmers keep the profits.

away in Washington State were being hit by high fuel prices—a phenomenon that affected the overall U.S. long-distance food distribution system. "People like the idea of a local farm," he said. That way, "they know where their food comes from."

ANOTHER INDOMITABLE AND INCREASINGLY DELECTABLE agricultural contribution in this region is the viticulture industry Thomas Jefferson started in the early 19th century. There are numerous notable vineyards along the length of the corridor, but within Orange County, one merits particular mention. A site that draws visitors from far and near to refresh body and spirit, Barboursville Vineyard carries one of those direct lines to the past that abound in the region. Thomas Jefferson not only offered viticulture advice but he designed the home of his dear friend James Barbour, governor of Virginia (1812-14), U.S. Senator (1815-25), and secretary of war (1825-28). Barbour planted grapes in the neighborhood as part of his enduring effort to make wine, which he called "the only antidote to the bane of whiskey." By many accounts, Governor Barbour's wine was exceptional. Legend has it that when a fire swept through his manor house on Christmas Day 1884, he instructed his staff to

VINTAGE-CAR OWNERS GATHER around the John Marshall Courthouse every Father's Day in Warrenton, Virginia, to show off their vehicles. It is only one of many community-rallying activities throughout the area that keep "Main Street America" alive.

MIDDLETOWN, MARYLAND
An aerial view, on Old Highway 40, also known as National Highway,
west of Frederick, Maryland. This beautiful historic landmark,
increasingly surrounded by modern growth, illustrates the importance
of managing growth and cluster development.

AT THE INN AT LITTLE WASHINGTON, in Washington, Virginia, owner Patrick O'Connell (opposite, top) smiles at the calm in his kitchen on the eve of Thanksgiving. The top-rated restaurant attracts a worldwide clientele while serving as a luxury hotel. The building across the street (opposite, bottom) was a tavern surveyed by the teenage George Washington. Combining history with innovations, such as the restaurant and hotel, has brought revenue to various locations in the region and helped preserve them.

carry the dinner table out to the lawn, so as not to disturb Christmas dinner. His guests continued eating and drinking while the fire raged, ultimately consuming the entire home and its contents.

THE CURRENT OWNERS SHARE BARBOUR'S PASSION FOR making wine. "In the early 1970s there was a wine being produced in Virginia," nationally acclaimed, Virginia-born viticulturist Lucie Morton remembered, "high alcohol content, sweet, and cheap. It wasn't necessarily what we'd call vintage these days, and even that was made from out-of-state grapes." But the area's winemaking industry has matured significantly. One advantage of the wine business, according to Morton, is that even a small acreage—if designed and managed correctly—can yield enough grapes to produce quite a lot of wines. By the mid-1970s, several wineries were beginning to prosper in the Piedmont in Virginia, Maryland, and Pennsylvania.

Not long after this time, the Italian wine mogul Gianni Zonin sent a skilled manager across the ocean to Virginia to try to create wine that could compete with products in Europe and California. The site chosen for this experiment was Barboursville, near the gutted shell of Jefferson's creation. "It took until the mid-1990s to produce a wine of quality, an age-worthy wine, in Virginia," says the current Barboursville Vineyards general manager and winemaker, Luca Paschina. "Before that, we had to understand the soil and the climate of the region; we had to learn how to grow grapes here, we had to learn how to prune the vines in the right way. All that took us two decades. If you think about it, in the famous wine regions of Italy and France, it took them centuries to work out what they should be doing, then each region settled on a few specialties."

Luca was a happy man the day he learned that the *Washington Post* was about to nominate his Octagon 2004, a red based on Merlot and Bordeaux grapes, as one of the very best wines of the year that their critic had tasted. "Now we know what to grow in Virginia," he said cheerfully, before conceding that in those two early decades "we made a lot of mistakes." Sometimes the mistakes were expensive. In the early 1990s, Paschina tore up "acres and acres" of vines after concluding they had the wrong rootstock and were too far apart. "There are so many variables," he said ruefully, "it's like rolling dice." Slowly, however, he and other winemakers along the corridor were coming to appreciate a basic truth: Just as the historic

AN OPEN LANDSCAPE
The gorgeous scene on Frogtown Road outside of Marshall, Virginia, is reminiscent of the kind of open landscape that draws tourists to view this countryside by car, on bicycle, and on foot.

A CHICKEN HOUSE ON WHEELS
(bottom) at Over The Grass Farm near
The Plains, Virginia, allows its residents
to move around regularly in the orchard,
where they can range freely on fresh ground.
Organically farmed, they are raised without
chemicals or herbicides. Pretty brown eggs
(right) are the result of such healthful living.

Old Carolina Road had to follow the fords on the rivers, the wine had to adapt to the land, and not the other way around.

Today, wineries have figured out ways to get more mileage out of their acreage through such techniques as vertical shoot positioning (VSP). This method of arranging the vines results in a "very neat, tightly managed canopy," according to Morton. Rather than allowing them to sprawl, VSP "is sustainable growth because you don't allow vines to grow uncontrolled, which makes them susceptible to disease, shades their neighbors, and leads to lack of uniformity." This training method also maximizes sunlight capture, yielding higher quality fruit. Morton designs vineyards with densely planted vines, situated in north-south rows to allow the maximum intensity of light to hit the vines from the east in the morning and the west in the afternoon. Winery workers pull leaves off the vines' eastern sides, permitting the gentle morning sun more direct access to the grapes; they leave the western leaves to shelter the grapes from searing afternoon heat.

"It's not the soil itself that's most important," reflected Paschina, "Most soils support grape growing. What's important is the landscape, the slope of the land, the microclimate of the vineyard."

Some of the many varieties of grapes now growing successfully in this region include the familiar Bordeaux red varieties: Cabernet Sauvignon, Cabernet Franc, Merlot and Petit Verdot; Burgundian white varieties: Chardonnay and Pinot Gris; and lesser-known and up-and-coming varieties such as Petit Manseng, Viognier, Tannat, and Fer Servadou from France; Graciano, Albariño, and Tempranillo from Spain; and Nebbiolo from Italy. In addition, Norton,

BUYING BOVINE SHARES
At Over The Grass Farm a dairyman heads his milk cow to the barn. It is possible to purchase a share of a cow—or a whole cow—so you get whatever amount of milk she produces that you have bargained for.

a varietal grown in Virginia as early as 1770, and the oldest North American grape grown today, is making a comeback.

Of the 30,000 cases of red, white and sparkling wine that are sold by Barboursville Vineyards each year, 40 percent are bought on site. In addition to the wines and the highly acclaimed restaurant, visitors are treated to the sights and scenery of a pastoral part of our American heritage. This approach—a homegrown and processed product sold in an inviting setting steeped in history—is an emerging pattern throughout the area. "I really think this agritourism is the way to go," said Morton, a consultant for the new vineyards sprouting up across the countryside. "Wineries in the Old Dominion, neighboring Maryland, and Pennsylvania will soon surpass 200. If a person can go and have nice wine in a nice setting with good food, what could be better? It's a model that's served Europe well, after all. Look at the Loire, or Tuscany. In Virginia, these family enterprises contribute several hundred million dollars to the state's economy through employment, taxes, and tourism."

The largest winery in the four-state region, Prince Michel Vineyard and Winery in Madison County, Virginia, supports independent winegrowers by buying grapes only from other Piedmont vineyards. Owners Terry and Kristin Holzmann are committed to ensuring that the cultural fabric of this heritage-rich countryside remains economically viable and preserved for generations to come. They have even created a special wine for the Journey Through Hallowed Ground Partnership, featuring a label painted by nationally acclaimed artist Antonia Walker, and they donate a percentage of the proceeds from each bottle to support the Partnership's ongoing conservation and educational efforts.

THE RICH, FERTILE LANDSCAPE THAT HAS HISTORICALLY supported vineyards, fruit orchards, dairy farms, and livestock farms has also created and sustained one of the finest equestrian industries in the country. The region has long been an agrarian-equestrian center, with a world-class breeding program and training for riders that has spawned Olympic competitors. Horses for farm work

HEALTH AID PRODUCTS PRODUCED at Stoneleigh Farms are made from honey and other natural ingredients. Items for sale include antibacterial hand soap, honey, and shampoo.

A YOUNG MEMBER OF THE FUTURE
Farmers of America brushes his pig before showing it at the annual Madison County Fair in Virginia. A blue ribbon winner, this animal is symbolic of the pride that originated in the character of the land and using it in the way for which it was originally intended and continues with the younger generation.

are also raised here. In 2006, the Virginia portion of the corridor was home to $800 million worth of horses. Loudoun and Fauquier Counties, which still have some rolling open land, form the heart of horse country, and have more than 30,000 horses combined, with more "equine operations" being added every year.

"Horses support a lot of people," said Will O'Keefe, executive director of the Westmoreland Davis Memorial Foundation, which operates the Morven Park Equestrian Center in Leesburg: "blacksmiths, grooms, feed suppliers, tack shops, vets, clothiers and more. When we host a big event here at Morven Park, every hotel and inn in Leesburg fills up, as well as the restaurants and stores. It's great for the economy." Virginians spent just under $100 million on feed and bedding in 2006, and another $92 million on harnesses and other equipment. "Even in trying times," says O'Keefe, "people are prepared to make sacrifices to keep horses."

Horses, like cattle, wineries, orchards, and all the other self-sustaining activities that keep a rural economy alive and vital, need land, something that is in increasingly short supply across Virginia but is still preserved in the Piedmont. "People in the horse industry now look at this region as about the only place where you can find land to operate on," said Chris Miller, president of the Piedmont Environmental Council, the leading comservation organization in the region. "There's just not enough space up north in places like New York and New Jersey anymore."

History resounds within this space. This region includes thousands of sites listed on the National Register of Historic Places, the largest collection of Civil War battlefields in the nation, 16 historic towns, and 49 historic districts. In the words of Yale University historian C. Vann Woodward, "This part of the country has soaked up more of the blood, sweat, and tears of American history than any other part of the country. It has bred more Founding Fathers, inspired more soaring hopes and ideals and witnessed more triumphs, failures, victories, and lost causes than any other place in the country."

While rich in heritage, the corridor continues to evolve and grow. Fortunately, here lives a community determined to ensure this heritage will be conserved for generations to come. According to a recent poll of residents throughout the four-state region, 88 percent stated that the historic and cultural assets of the region were extremely important to their quality of life, and 91 percent stated that this heritage was very important to the region's economy.

"The dedication to sustaining the stories, the ideals and the land of our Founding Fathers is as real and as vibrant a call to the members of this community as, perhaps, to those who first trod this land and called for democracy and civil accountability," said the founder and president of the Journey Through Hallowed Ground Partnership, Cate Magennis Wyatt. "Our partners and the citizens throughout this region, over many generations, take this duty seriously."

Fortunately, as the preceding pages may demonstrate, this is a land where, throughout history, people have defended their way of life, stretching back to the Monocan Indians, who greeted John Smith with a shower of arrows and subsequently managed to more than survive against overwhelming odds. Others have continued the tradition: the minutemen who gathered at Culpeper on that October day in 1775; the Confederate soldier who told his

captors that he fought "because you're here"; the brave Dutton sisters of 1860s Waterford who published their antislavery newspaper in the midst of the Civil War; Charlie Houston, the first African-American attorney to argue a major case in a southern courtroom; W. E. B. Du Bois, whose efforts helped lay the groundwork for the 20th-century civil rights movement; Jennie Dean, who founded the Manassas Industrial School; and the dedicated conservationists, farmers, elected officials, business owners, educators, and historians fighting for the community today.

"Each generation of citizens who lived within this region placed life and livelihood on the line as they sought, as they created, and as they protected the nascent notions of democracy," says Wyatt. "By establishing a sustainable means of supporting the heritage and cultural traditions within the Journey Through Hallowed Ground— the birthplace of the American ideal—citizens honor the sacrifices of those who preceded us. We invite every American to join this effort to ensure our ideals are available to inform future generations."

In different ways, and for different reasons, this is truly Hallowed Ground for every one of us.

AT THE BARBOURSVILLE WINERY IN Orange County, the Octagon label (opposite, top) on the bottle signifies the house that Thomas Jefferson designed for James Barbour, an early governor of Virginia. The Octagon's ruins still stand on the property (below). Visitors in the tasting room (opposite, bottom) sample a vintage selection.

After years of development, Barboursville Vineyards and others produce award-winning, world-class wines. Also, the proximity to Montpelier, some ten miles north on Route 20, makes it an easy drive for heritage tourists as well as those interested in the region's relatively new wine industry.

CONGREGATING TO CAROL
On the main street of Frederick, Maryland, carolers in period costume celebrate the Christmas season. The first Saturday evening of each month is devoted to activities designed to encourage enjoyment of downtown. In recent years, there has been a major—and successful— effort to rebuild and reinvigorate the historic downtown area.

EPILOGUE

WHAT IF? This is a question we rarely need ask when it comes to considering the creation of America and our American ideals. We are spared this ultimatum because those who had to address this question did so by placing life and livelihood on the line to answer it. Today, we have the remarkable good fortune to reap the benefits of their hard-fought and often perilous battles.

As these pages reveal, we are the beneficiaries of those who stood face to face with the question "What if?" W. E. B. Du Bois saw racial injustice in 1906 and chose to convene the first American meeting of the Niagara Conference in Harpers Ferry. Seminal in itself, this meeting led to the creation of the NAACP, yet as he planned this meeting he made sure the participants walked from Storer College to the nearby Murphy family farm, the site of the historic fort where John Brown's quest to free four million enslaved blacks 50 years earlier reached its bloody climax. Once there they removed their shoes and socks to walk the field, honor the hallowed ground, and participate in a ceremony of remembrance.

Every step within the Journey Through Hallowed Ground is just as inspired. Generation after generation, the citizens who lived within this swath of land, from Monticello, in Virginia, to Gettysburg, Pennsylvania, chose to address or were most inconveniently confronted with the question *What if?* Fortunately for us all, because of their many acts of selflessness, the fundamental *American ideals* were born, sustained, challenged, nurtured, and brought to fruition. Here we have shared but a few of the stories of the heralded and the unknown, men and women of many races—Indians, Europeans, and Africans—each of whom stood squarely

before the daunting questions: *What should I do? And what happens if I don't? What will happen to my family?* and had to determine for themselves the right path to take. Some knew that the answer would result in the creation of this country. Others chose the path to sustain this country. In most but not all cases, they chose the path they believed was for the benefit of all; their actions have paved the enduring road toward freedom and democracy along which we journey today.

Thomas Jefferson, James Madison, James Monroe, and John Marshall came largely from the comfortable society, yet each chose to take up arms against his then sovereign nation. Had they lost this battle their acts would have been considered treasonous, with a ruinous and perhaps lethal outcome. As we study their acts and their values we are reminded of the difficulties they faced with unparalleled courage.

As you absorb Kenneth Garrett's images, and read Andrew Cockburn's text, we invite you to ask yourself, "*What if?*" And then, ask yourself, "*What would I have done?*" These are not easy questions, and the answers should not come quickly.

In thinking about these questions you are invited to place your feet in the boots of those who have gone before you, to experience the "Birthplace of the American Ideal" and appreciate that our American ideals are just that—ideals. If not embraced and if not honored, respected, and protected, we might all, again, be faced with *What if?*

Cate Magennis Wyatt
President
The Journey Through Hallowed
Ground Partnership

ABOUT THE JOURNEY THROUGH HALLOWED GROUND PARTNERSHIP

The Journey Through Hallowed Ground Partnership is a nonprofit organization dedicated to raising national awareness of the unparalleled history in the region, which generally follows the Old Carolina Road (Rt. 15/231) from Gettysburg, through Maryland, to Monticello in Albemarle County, Virginia. From its communities, farms, businesses, and heritage sites, we have an opportunity to celebrate and preserve this vital fabric of America.

The Journey Through Hallowed Ground Partnership is dedicated to encouraging both Americans and world visitors to *Take the Journey* to appreciate, respect, and experience this cultural landscape that shares the stories of *"Where America Happened."*

We are doing this by:

- Building and supporting a strong network of local, regional, and national partners who work collaboratively to develop a common vision for the conservation and enhancement of the scenic, historic, recreational, cultural, and natural characteristics of the region. Among our efforts is the creation of The Journey Through Hallowed Ground National Heritage Area, legislation for which recently passed in the U.S. House of Representatives.
- Developing educational programs for students and teachers so that all can learn from the stories of the noble and the ordinary citizens who did extraordinary things to shape this nation.
- Creating heritage tourism programs to increase civic engagement and to make it easier for citizens and visitors to "Take the Journey" to our state and national parks, historic downtown communities, museums, and heritage sites.
- Working in partnership with every local, state, and nationally elected body within the region to create national and international programs to recognize the critical importance of sharing our American heritage.

For more information on how you can become involved, please visit *www.HallowedGround.org*

QUICK FACTS

- 11,000 years of Native American history
- 400 years of European, American, and African American history
- Nine U.S. presidential homes, including Thomas Jefferson's Monticello, James Madison's Montpelier, James Monroe's Oak Hill and Ashlawn Highland, the Dwight David Eisenhower Farm and Zachary Taylor's home, John F. Kennedy's country home, Herbert Hoover's cabin, and Theodore Roosevelt's Pine Knot cabin
- The home of Chief Justice John Marshall, and that of one of the finest arbiters of justice, Gen. George C. Marshall, who penned the Marshall Plan from his home, in Leesburg, Va.
- Two World Heritage sites
- 49 National Historic Districts
- More than a million acres on the National Register of Historic Places
- The largest collection of Civil War battlefields in America
- The greatest concentration of Rural Historic Districts in America
- 16 National Historic Landmarks
- Numerous scenic rivers and landscapes
- 13 National Parks units
- Significant cultural and agricultural destinations, including vineyards, pick-your-own farms, and equestrian events

INDEX

Journey Through Hallowed Ground

•	Populated place
ⓘ	City with visitor center
Gettysburg*	City with Main Street programs
	Presidential site
	Battle site
	Historic site
	Cemetery
15	Journey route
81	Interstate highway
50	Divided highway
66	Other road
	Railroad
	Scenic byway
	Appalachian National Scenic Trail
	Chesapeake and Ohio Canal
	Mosby Heritage Area
	State boundary
	County boundary
CLARKE	County name
	State and National parkland

Statute Miles   0   25

Kilometers   0   25

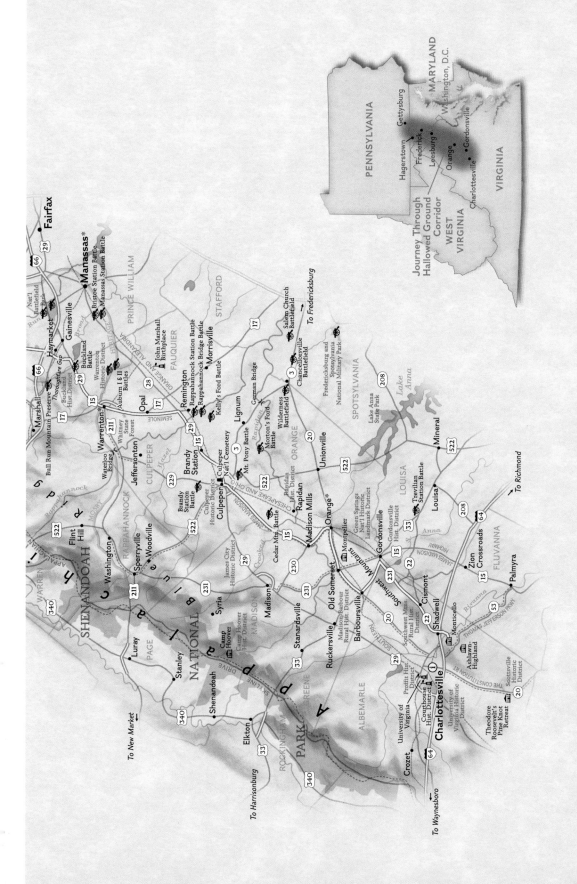

Journey Through Hallowed Ground Corridor

PENNSYLVANIA

MARYLAND

Washington, D.C.

Hagerstown
Gettysburg
Frederick
Leesburg
Orange
Gordonsville

WEST VIRGINIA

VIRGINIA

Charlottesville

Fairfax

Manassas*

MARYLAND

66
29

Haymarket
Gainesville
Thoroughfare Gap
Buckland Battle
Warrenton Historic District
Bristoe Station Battle
Manassas Station Battle

PRINCE WILLIAM

STAFFORD

Bull Run Mountain Preserve
Marshall
66

Auburn I & II Battles

John Marshall Birthplace

17

Morrisville

Salem Church Battlefield

To Fredericksburg

29
15
211

Waterloo Bridge

Whitney State Forest
Jeffersonton

FAUQUIER

28
17

Opal

Remington
Rappahannock Station Battle
Rappahannock Bridge Battle
Kelly's Ford Battle

Warrenton

German Bridge

3

Chancellorsville Battlefield

Fredericksburg and Spotsylvania National Military Park

Lake Anna

522
Flint Hill

Washington

Sperryville
Woodville

CULPEPER

229

522

Brandy Station Battle

Culpeper Historic District

Culpeper Nat'l Cemetery

Mt. Pony Battle

Morton's Ford Battle

Wilderness Battlefield

Unionville

Lake Anna State Park

SPOTSYLVANIA

Mineral

522

James City Historic District

RAPPAHANNOCK

29

Brandy Station

15

3

522

Rapidan Hist. District

ORANGE

20

522

208

SHENANDOAH NATIONAL PARK

211

231

Luray

Camp Hoover
Camp Hoover Hist. District

Syria

Madison

230

Cedar Mtn. Battle

15

Madison Mills

Rapidan

Orange*

Montpelier

Green Springs Nat'l Historic Landmark District

LOUISA

Trevilian Station Battle

Gordonsville Hist. District

Louisa

208

PAGE

Stanley

MADISON

231

Old Somerset

Southwest Mtns.

231

Gordonsville

33

Anna

Zion Crossroads

15

JAMES MADISON HIGHWAY

64

To Richmond

Madison-Barbour Rural Hist. District

Barboursville

22

Cismont

Palmyra

FLUVANNA

Shenandoah

Stanardsville

33

Ruckersville

20

Southwest Mtn. Rural Hist. District

22

Shadwell

Monticello

Rivanna

53

THOMAS JEFFERSON PKWY

Elkton

ROCKINGHAM MTS.

GREENE

29

Profitt Hist. District

1

Courthouse Hist. District

ALBEMARLE

University of Virginia

Charlottesville

University of Virginia Historic District

Ashlawn-Highland

Theodore Roosevelt's Pine Knot Retreat

Scottsville Historic District

20

340

Crozet

64

To Waynesboro

To New Market

To Harrisonburg

340

33

WARREN

APPALACHIAN TRAIL

BLUE RIDGE

ORANGE AND ALEXANDRIA

CHESAPEAKE AND OHIO

JAMES MADISON

SEMINOLE

Rappahannock

Hazel

Rapidan

Broad

Crooked

THE CONSTITUTION RT.

ACKNOWLEDGMENTS

As Daniel Jordan, president of the Thomas Jefferson Foundation, observed earlier in this book, our country was founded on the good fortune of "the constellation of leaders" who all happened to reside within this swath of land. As he states, had the events of the late 1770s unfolded a few years later, "you wouldn't have had that same constellation in the Piedmont." For reasons unexplained, but with equal admiration, this book is dedicated to the unprecedented constellation of individuals who reside within the Piedmont and have chosen to create The Journey Through Hallowed Ground Partnership. If not for the constancy and vision of the citizen leaders within this area, each of whom has given selflessly as stewards, these scared places, these stories, and the very cultural fabric of this country would have unraveled long ago.

Among the early visionaries in this endeavor we wish to acknowledge: Jacqueline Mars whose many gifts include the inspiration for this book; Frederick and Diana Prince, who saw, long before many others, the need to create the JTHG Partnership; Kristin Pauly, executive director of the Prince Charitable Trusts, for her puissant guidance; the inimitable Robert H. Smith, himself a true American hero, whose vision, acumen, commitment, and generosity epitomize the Founding Fathers' ideals; Cornelia Keller, our friend and neighbor, who unfailingly prods us with unerring insights; and Mark and Ann Kington, Dorothy and Jonathon Rintel, Schuyler Richardson, Tom Edmonds, and Virginia Warner—visionaries each in their own right.

Thomas Jefferson Foundation's president, Dan Jordan, has demanded rigorous academic analysis of our Founding Fathers, while vice president, Kat Imhoff, served as the first chair of the JTHG Partnership. Michael Quinn, president of the Montpelier Foundation, Richard Moe, president of The National Trust for Historic Preservation, Peter Brink, Robert Nieweg, and their entire organizations have brought a level of reach and determined resolve, which sustains our every effort.

Jim Lighthizer, Jim Campi, and the team of professionals at the Civil War Preservation Trust and the Trust for Public Land have combined forces to ensure the endurance of our cultural landscape for generations. Chris Miller, president of the Piedmont Environmental Council, Doug Larson, Mike Dehart, and the entire PEC Board and organization have likewise led unparalleled conservation efforts. Our partners within the National Park Service, including the magnificent superintendents, have been invaluable.

We especially thank Geraldine Brooks, the Pulitzer Prize-winning novelist who has graced these pages with her thoughtful foreword, and Andrew Cockburn, for his inimitable prose. We express enormous gratitude to Ken Garrett who has spent three years bringing this book to fruition. Additionally, if not for the generosity and talents of Nick, Mary Lynn, and Jack Kotz, this book would not have been created. It has been an honor and a pleasure to work with the team of professionals within the National Geographic Society, with special thanks to the unflinching patience of Barbara Brownell Grogan, Susan Straight, and Peggy Archambault.

As this book goes to print, the Journey Through Hallowed Ground Partnership awaits an act of Congress to designate the Journey Through Hallowed Ground National Heritage Area. This multiyear effort has been driven by the tireless efforts of Representative Frank Wolf, Senator John Warner, their respective outstanding staffs, and the pro bono legal services of Don Pongrace, Katherine Brodie, and their colleagues at Akin Gump Strauss Hauer & Feld LLP. For these many efforts, we are eternally grateful.

MAIN STREET THRIVES in Leesburg, Virginia. Throngs of spectators watch the annual Fourth of July parade.

Among the many additional contributors to the effort to sustain our heritage, we wish to sincerely acknowledge the gifts of the countless educators with whom we are blessed to work. To name but a few: Dan Kent, Rob Hallock, Dean Herrin, W. Brown Morton III, Marye Griffith, Bill Brazier, Ken Bassett, Bev Blois, Shelley Mastran, Rich Gillespie, David Porter, and Dennis Campbell,

As is often the case, those who have labored the longest are often mentioned last. Among those would be our additional trustees: Arthur Arundel, Cheryl Kilday, Alice Estrada, John Fieseler, Kevin Fry, Gilbert M. Grosvenor, Kathleen Kilpatrick, and David Williams; advisers: Bill Backer, Susan Eisenhower, Dr. John Latschar, Ron Maxwell, Ed McMahon, and Bessie Carter; and the JTHG Partnership Team: Olwen Pongrace, Beth Erickson, Jaime McClung, Jennifer Moore, Lauren Searl, Paul McDonald, Angela Stokes, Ed Lehmann, Abigail DeLashmutt, and Lorinda Laryea.

We like to think of this effort as the creation of legacy, which in years to come will have many asking, "Who made this gift possible?" The short answer is: these individuals, and so many more. Each of whom has given time, talents, financial support, and dreams to sustain our American Heritage so that future generations may benefit by its inspiring stories and landscape.

Cate Magennis Wyatt
President
The Journey Through Hallowed
Ground Partnership

JOURNEY THROUGH HALLOWED GROUND

ANDREW COCKBURN
PHOTOGRAPHY BY KENNETH GARRETT

Published by the National Geographic Society
John M. Fahey, Jr., President and Chief Executive Officer
Gilbert M. Grosvenor, Chairman of the Board
Tim T. Kelly, President, Global Media Group
Nina D. Hoffman, Executive Vice President;
   President, Book Publishing Group

Prepared by the Book Division
Kevin Mulroy, Senior Vice President and Publisher
Leah Bendavid-Val, Director of Photography
   Publishing and Illustrations
Marianne R. Koszorus, Director of Design
Barbara Brownell Grogan, Executive Editor
Elizabeth Newhouse, Director of Travel Publishing
Carl Mehler, Director of Maps

Staff for This Book
Susan Straight, Project Editor
Judith Klein, Susan Tyler Hitchcock, Contributing
   Editors
Peggy Archambault, Art Director
Trudy Pearson, Researcher
Robert Waymouth, Illustrations Specialist
Al Morrow, Design Assistant
Michael Horenstein, Production Manager
Connie D. Binder, Indexer
Tiffin Thompson, Intern

Jennifer A. Thornton, Managing Editor
Gary Colbert, Production Director
Meredith C. Wilcox, Administrative Director, Illustrations

Manufacturing and Quality Management
Christopher A. Liedel, Chief Financial Officer
Phillip L. Schlosser, Vice President
John T. Dunn, Technical Director
Chris Brown, Director
Maryclare Tracy, Manager
Nicole Elliott, Manager

Founded in 1888, the National Geographic Society is one of the largest nonprofit scientific and educational organizations in the world. It reaches more than 285 million people worldwide each month through its official journal, *National Geographic*, and its four other magazines; the National Geographic Channel; television documentaries; radio programs; films; books; videos and DVDs; maps; and interactive media. National Geographic has funded more than 8,000 scientific research projects and supports an education program combating geographic illiteracy.

For more information, please call 1-800-NGS LINE (647-5463) or write to the following address:

National Geographic Society
1145 17th Street N.W.
Washington, D.C. 20036-4688 U.S.A.

Visit us online at www.nationalgeographic.com

For information about special discounts for bulk purchases, please contact National Geographic Books Special Sales: ngspecsales@ngs.org

For rights or permissions inquiries, please contact National Geographic Books Subsidiary Rights: ngbookrights@ngs.org

Photo credit: 160, Jack Kotz

ISBN 978-1-4262-0350-3 (regular)
ISBN 978-1-4262-0351-0 (deluxe)

Library of Congress Cataloging-in-Publication Data available upon request.

Printed in U.S.